THE SEVEN P.

OF THE KINGDOM

Roger Penney

THE SEVEN PARABLES OF THE KINGDOM

Roger Penney

Second edition

PREFACE

I have to thank my colleague Fraser for the work he does guiding us through the complexities of I.T. This is why we are CRF Publishes. Without C. and F. I would simply be an unsuccessful writer hopelessly trying to interest disinterested and bored publishers and literary agents in my manuscripts. They would in addition be badly typed and badly presented.

In the case of this particular study I also wish to thank my friend Simon Marshall for his careful and thorough proof reading and his advice. He was quite right, as proof readers usually are but he went the other mile (and more) and made many helpful suggestions. More of my paragraphs than I car to think about would have been hopelessly confusing for the reader if Simon had not strongly advised me to rewrite.

Writing Biblical exposition is doubly difficult because of the amount of research one has to do. On has need of the Concordance. You know the passage you want. You are quite certain it is in Isaiah, and yet you cannot find it. At last, when you have almost given up hope, you find it in Amos or in Joel instead.

The idea of writing Biblical exposition is first of all an expression of one's own love for the Word of God. How clear are the words of the Psalm:

"The Law of the Lord is perfect, converting the soul."

"The testimony of the Lord is sure, making wise the simple.

The statutes of the Lord are right, rejoicing the heart."

"The Commandment of the Lord is pure enlightening the eyes.

The fear of the Lord is clean, enduring forever."

"The judgments of the Lord are true and righteous altogether.

More to be desired are they than gold. Yea than much fine gold.

Sweeter also than honey and the honeycomb."(Ps.19:7-9)

Secondly one hopes to leave something to encourage others and to give them something to think about to meditate upon. I do not expect readers to agree with me. I may be wrong in many of the points I make. However if I have helped someone else to think things out for themselves then I have achieved something small and good for eternity.

Thirdly and most important of all one hopes that in some way these lines I have written will give glory to God and honour to our Lord Jesus Christ. They may even help to bring some dear folk to Him for their Salvation.

CONTENTS

INTRODUCTION

Remote Background

There are several occasions when God and man meet on or around mountains. By contrast chapter thirteen of Matthew starts with the Lord Jesus on the sea shore, seated in a boat, with the multitude before Him on the land. This is significant as are the previous scenes. Indeed these, prior to the scene we are considering at the beginning of chapter thirteen, give us an overview of God's dealings with the world and with the people in it.

The occasion on Mount Sinai after God had rescued His people from slavery in Egypt, saw Moses going up to God. (Ex. 20:9-15.) Having been called by God, Moses then went up the mountain to meet with God and to receive the Law. We need to note that immediately before this they were offered an agreement with God. Moses had previously gone up to the Mountain. God had said to him. "If you will obey My voice, and keep My covenant, then you shall be a peculiar treasure unto Me above all people." The reply of the whole nation to this was a fateful one. "All that the Lord has spoken we will do." (vv5-8)

In Matthew's Gospel, at the beginning of the Lord's ministry, we find Him with the people. He called some of his disciples and then, a little later went about all Galilee teaching in the synagogues and healing the crowds of sick people. We may then turn to the situation which Matthew tells us about at the beginning of his chapter thirteen. The Lord is seated in a boat which has been pulled out a little from the shore, the better to give him a view of the crowd. They by contrast are on the shore, on the dry land.

No action, no word of the Lord Jesus was ever by accident. Everything was done deliberately and to the glory of His Father. Everything was also done to demonstrate a particular significance.

So it was that He first "sat by the sea". When, "great multitudes were gathered together unto Him," He then changed his position relative to the crowd and to the seashore. This move to sit in a boat is remarkable in that He thus separated himself, both from the crowds and from the land.

Superficially this move was to make His message more accessible to the people so He needed the boat as a platform so from it he could see the widest extent of the crowd. This is certainly true but it is not all. The move served, slightly but effectively to separate Himself, from the crowd. It also gives us something to understand about His relation to the crowds and to the people generally. He was, and is, among us. He was, and is, a person separated from all other human beings. First he is God the Son that makes Him a person different and separate from all others. Secondly He was, of course, sinless, completely and utterly. Thirdly He spoke the words of God directly from Himself and from His Father. We can only pass on what we learn of Him and from Him. Finally His attributes as Deity meant that He knew all things including the terrible fact that He was to be crucified and was to "be made sin". He had always before Him this mission, the cross was a reality which he lived with permanently.

The Sea is often a picture of the peoples and nations of the world. In Daniel chapter seven we read of how, "the four winds of heaven strove upon the great sea. And four great beasts came up from the sea, diverse one from another." (Dan.7:2) Here in Matthew in chapter thirteen we see that the Lord has come down to the multitudes. This was a Jewish crowd but we may also understand that He had come for all peoples but first to the Jews, to Israel His earthly people.

Crowds are fickle. He had shown Himself one with them already but, as time went on and the hostility of the Pharisees became more organized it was soon to draw in the priests and others into the conspiracy to destroy Him. So too would the once enthusiastic crowds begin to have doubts about Him while some, like the blind man's parents, would already have begun to dissociate themselves from Him through fear of the authorities. (cf. Jn. 9:18-23.)

The Immediate Background

The cry of the Lord Jesus is heart rending in its longing and in the realisation that the Lord knew what it would cost Him to bring about the salvation of the downtrodden, the poor, the fatherless and the widow. At the very end of chapter eleven He uttered the words which encapsulate the longing which is expressed in the call to the lost to come to Him for salvation.

"Come unto Me all ye that labour and are heavy laden and I will give you rest. Take my yoke upon you and learn of me; for I am meek and lowly in heart and you shall find rest unto your souls. For My yoke is easy and my burden is light." (Mt.11:27-29.) How much more loving, how much more enlightening and uplifting? And with what longing these words are expressed. How much better they are than the harsh call of Marx to revolution or the siren song of capitalism to lives of pleasure, wage slavery and consumerism. How the Lord Jesus understands and calls on the exploited and despised masses to come to Him and find rest.

Chapter twelve opens with the disciples on the way to the synagogue where the Lord Jesus was obviously expected and where He was to meet with the man with the withered hand. We remember that the lord Jesus, with His disciples usually travelled on foot. He was a poor man among the poor. That is all the rich and the powerful were able to see. That is all those in authority understood. A poor man among poor men. The intellectuals saw it

8

as an insult that He should take it upon himself to teach people and even to presume to teach them who had attended the schools, our equivalent of the Universities, in Jerusalem.

So the disciples were weary and it may have been sometime since they had eaten. For that reason they were able to take advantage of the law which allowed travelers to help themselves to fruit or grain growing alongside the roadway. However this was a sin in the eyes of the Pharisees, for that day was Sabbath. It was a holy day when no one should work. At least that is what they thought.

The Pharisees believed they had a law that was handed down from Moses by word of mouth and only the rabbis understood it. They believed it was as important as the Torah the Law of Moses, the Written Law. If you took grain, rubbed it in your hands to separate the grain from the husks then blew on it to get rid of the chaff then you were reaping, threshing and winnowing. This, on the Sabbath, they argued was doing work and so was against the Law. Indeed it was three varieties of work and so that much more deplorable.

The Law was really quite simple it said. "When you come into the standing corn of your neighbour you may pluck the ears of corn with thine hand." You were not allowed to take a reaping hook to the corn that would have been to take more than you needed to simply alleviate the pangs of hunger while on a journey. (Deut.23:25.)

Of course the Pharisees wanted to discredit the Lord Jesus, they felt threatened by Him and so the actions of the disciples seemed an opportunity to attack His teaching and His example. They had not, however, thought this through. The Lord gave two examples which showed that it was not illegal to do what the disciples were doing on the Sabbath.

First He gave the example of King David. Saul wanted to kill David. As with the Pharisees and the Lord Jesus the motive for this was jealousy. David had to run for his life and with his followers entered the Tabernacle and was given the holy bread which was laid up on the golden table before God. Only the priests were allowed to eat it, but the priest understood David's plight and gave the bread to him and to his men. (1Sam.21:1-6. Lev.24:5-9.)

In giving this example, though His critics may have not realised it, He was showing that, like David, He was a King in rejection. He too was the true King of Israel. Humanly speaking his mother and the man, Joseph, who was his earthly father, were both descended from King David. Herod had tried to have him killed as a baby and the Pharisees were looking for means by which they might bring down his popularity and His influence with the people. "He came to His own (things) and His own (people) received Him not." (Jn. 1:11.) He was despised and rejected of men." (Isaiah 53:3)

Next the Lord referred His critics to the Law again and to the work of the priests in the temple, and the performance of the rite of circumcision on the Sabbath. (Num. 28:9, 10. See also Jn.7:22, 23.) Clearly the offering of sacrifices was work as was circumcising a child at eight days old. (Lev. 12:3.) There was nothing the Pharisees could say regarding this so they were effectively silenced. For the time being that is.

If the above criticism was opportunistic then the next seems probably to have been purposefully planned and set up. The way Matthew presents his account indicates that this is so. The use of the word, 'behold' is significant for a start. It marks out the man as significant. On a human level he was significant to the Pharisees, for they wished to trap the Lord. The whole scene was a planned set up. "He went into their synagogue and behold, there was a man which had his hand withered. And they asked Him, saying, 'is it lawful to heal on the Sabbath,' that they might accuse Him." The question was a leading on and the man, clearly known was the bait for their trap. They knew that the Lord never turned anyone away who needed Him or what he had to give.

As before the Lord answered the carping of the Pharisees by reference to the Law of Moses. If it was lawful to lift, or to help lift, a sheep stuck in a hole and free it; then because a man was more important than a sheep it was lawful to heal him. Indeed, as the Lord pointed out, the wider principle was that it was always lawful to do good, whatever the occasion.

We see next a consummation where the attempted persecution of the Lord reached a climax and the hostility now involved all his enemies plotting together. At first they had merely murmured, In this chapter (12) we see, first an opportunistic attempt against Him. Next the attempt is planned and set up. Finally in verse 14 we read that "the Pharisees went out and held a council against Him, how they might destroy Him. "This is no longer localised but it seems as if the hostility has spread and this is a full council of the leading Pharisees. That their aim was to 'destroy' Him tells us clearly that they wanted to kill him. The same word is used in chapter two where the family flee for refuge into Egypt to avoid Herod who wished to 'destroy' Him. (2:13.) Also in chapter eight the disciples in the boat cried out to the Lord to save them or they would 'perish' here the same word is translated differently, but the meaning is the same.

However the chapter goes on leading us to see the cosmic element of this conflict. Satan had not given up. Having tried to subvert the Lord and His mission in chapter four by his testing of the Lord in the wilderness, he also went on to attempt physical destruction by means of a tempest caused by an earthquake. The word for 'tempest' here is 'seismos'. We find Satan using all the means in

11

his power to ruin or kill the Lord Jesus. From chapter twelve onwards he changes from direct intervention and uses human instruments for his purposes. Very carefully and cunningly he orchestrated the interplay of the Jewish sects to bring them together against the Lord and then to play on their fears of Rome and the weakness of the Roman Procurator and his fear of his wife's uncle, the Emperor Tiberius.

With the Pharisees plotting against Him the Lord Jesus withdrew Himself and forbad people to "make Him known". He referred to Isaiah's prophecy and then, when he had healed a blind and dumb man and the Pharisees had gone one step more in their rejection of Him; He raised the question of the two kingdoms. Since the Pharisees accused him of doing His miracles, "by Beelzebub, prince of the demons," He went on to show that Satan's kingdom would then be divided. He said. "But if I cast our demons by the Spirit of God, then the Kingdom of God is come unto you."

At this stage of the narrative there is a clear division between the forces of light and the forces of darkness; between the Kingdom of God and the Kingdom of the Devil. The chapter then concludes with the Lord, together with His disciples, in a house. He having first left a warning with the nation that worse was to come upon them. This is a fixed principle that if the evil spirit is cast out because of the work of God the Holy Spirit but where a true change of heart and life does not occur, then the original evil spirit returns with seven others worse than Himself. We may see the present hatred against Israel and their sufferings over the years as an outworking of this principle. The spirit, as it were of Hitlerism, was cast out. However the spirits of ant-Jewish hatred are returning seven-fold into the world, particularly among the nations of the Arab world.

The Lord at this time changed his previous openness for what appears to be secretiveness. It only appears so for though He told those He healed "that they should not make Him known." There was of course no possibility of everyone who came into the 'joy of the Lord' keeping quiet about it. Maybe He wished the Pharisees to ease up on their vehement hatred or, more likely, He did not want people to hear of Him second hand, as it were. Rather He would consider it better that they came to see him heal and to hear His Word.

Elsewhere He forbids people he has blessed or healed to acknowledge that He is the Christ. We may understand this only in the light of the wider context. Matthew tells us that: "Then charged He His disciples that they should tell no man that He was Jesus the Christ." (Matthew 16:20. See also Luke 9:21.) Daniel also tells us that the sixty nine sevens of years would end with the revelation of "Messiah the Prince". It was only when the Lord, at the end of His public ministry, fulfilled Zechariah chapter nine and verse nine by riding into Jerusalem on "a colt the foal of an ass," that the Lord publicly declared Himself to be Messiah the Prince and so also fulfilling the prophecy of Daniel. Had He done so earlier he would have made nonsense of the prophecies.

On hearing of His next healing of the blind and dumb man, the Pharisees argued that his healings were done by the power of Satan. The Lord easily turned the argument back on them by asking how Satan could be working against himself if he were indeed working on both sides. He referred to the principle and challenged them. "He that is not with me is against Me; and He that gathers not with Me scatters." (Matthew 12:30)

Following this it is clear that the lines were drawn. The Lord further warned them that if they accused Him of working by the power of the Devil then they had committed the unforgiveable sin, that of blasphemy since they were in fact saying that the Holy Spirit, by Whom the power of the Lord was working, was the Devil.

He then warned them that if an evil spirit was exorcised then if the person who had been under the control of the spirit did not actually follow the lord as a result, then it might well come back bringing seven other spirits worse than the original one. There are times when people who are challenged by the Gospel, clean up their lives but where there is no real turning of the heart and mind to the Lord Jesus, they end up worse than they had been before.

As far as this is concerned it is a general principle but in particular it was applied to Israel at the time and for the future. Messiah has, "come to His own (things) and His own people received Him not." (Jn.1:11.) Some years later the Romans came and burned the temple taking many Jews captive and killing many others. The spirit of idolatry had been cast out but the hypocrisy of the Pharisees and the carnal frauds of the priests and their materialism all meant that evil was spreading and getting worse. The climax of that evil, evil directly orchestrated by Satan, was the blasphemy against the Holy Spirit and the attempted judicial murder of the Lord Jesus.

Another principle He showed them and one which we also ought to heed was when, while in the house with His disciples, his mother and his brothers expected Him to come out to them simply because of who they were. One does not expect the Commander of an army to go home in the middle of a battle in order to see to family matters. Indeed, I have a letter from 1917 at the start of the Battle of Cambrai where my father's mother had requested that my father (a British soldier) come home to attend his father's funeral. His immediate superior wrote to my grandmother saying that her son was required for urgent military duties and could not be spared.

We see the same principle at work here on a vaster, cosmic battleground. We are reminded of this when we read that no natural sweetness was to be used in the sacrifices and the service of God in the Tabernacle and in the Temple. "You shall burn no leaven nor any honey in any offering of the Lord made by fire." (Lev.2:11.) The Lord put it a different and more direct way when speaking of natural relations He said, "he that loves father or mother more than me is not worthy of me." (Mt. 10:37.)

There is nothing new under the sun. Still, in our own time, the same principles are in operation. Where the Judeo-Christian system of morality and belief has been in operation for many years there has been a government and a culture more just and more benign than in those countries where such a system has been unknown. There cruelty and arbitrary rule have been the norm. Now that in our western society evolution has given sinful men the excuse to parrot that 'science has disproved the Bible' we find our culture spiraling downwards into anarchy and into depravity. We are becoming worse than the closed mind or tyrannical political systems where God's law has never been known, or if known, never honoured.

Christians are now spoken against and are vilified or ridiculed while those who slander us try in vain to cobble together a pattern for society which only looks to materialism and the love of mammon on which to base their principles of government. This world view is materialistic and the whole shoddy tapestry is held together by the rotten threads of human wisdom which is no wisdom at all but a lurch from one expedient to another.

Politics today all over the world, in the ruins of the Judeo-Christian system or in the closed mind materialist Islamic system or in whatever world view the particular society may hold, is in turmoil. There is no real supreme authority. There are no moral absolutes

15

but everyman "does that which is right in his own eyes" and the result is anarchy with factional interests vying for supremacy, and no one capable of arbitrating. The Book of Judges, long ago, gave a terrifying picture of a society in dissolution.

The Cosmic Battle Ground

The parables which follow are a complete group. There are seven which is God's number of completeness and finality. They are about rule, about conquest, and about the ongoing struggle of right against wrong, of good against evil and of God against Satan. Before we can look at the parables themselves we must define the terms, 'The Kingdom of God' and 'The Kingdom of Heaven'.

We have to recognise that human opinions do not matter. It is what the Bible says about this that really matters and which defines the meanings of words and phrases. We have Peter to thank for setting out this principle of interpretation. He wrote as follows. "Knowing this first, that no prophecy of the Scripture is its own interpretation." In other words we find that in the Bible there are other passages which throw light upon an issue and so these ought to be taken into consideration when we try to understand that particular issue. Far too many preachers and would-be teachers give us the dubious benefit of their own, private thoughts. These only lead to confusion.

There are two main possibilities with regard to the Kingdom. Either the two phrases, Kingdom of God and Kingdom of Heaven are different or they are the same. On the other hand there is always a chance that they may be like partly overlapping circles. It may be that they are similar but if we argue that they are different we have to be able to show how they are different and what those differences are. We also have to decide how to apply our

16

interpretation of these two Kingdoms and the conflict between them.

The general idea and the explanation offered in the schools is that parables, literally 'things thrown alongside,' give illustrations which make the teaching easier to understand. When we look at the text, and examine it closely, we find that that is not the case. It is rather that people, trying to be clever take the superficial as the meaning when in fact there is a deeper, symbolic meaning. That is why it is important to define the meanings of the Kingdoms and to ascertain whose kingdoms.

Nebuchadnezzar had a dream involving a tree. In the dream, "a watcher and a holy one came down from heaven. He cried aloud and said thus. 'Hew down the tree and cut off his branches, shake off his leaves and scatter his fruit'." The tree had been a refuge for animals in its shade and for birds in its branches. Yet, "by decree of the watchers and by demand of the holy ones," the tree was preserved while the king was to become like a beast for the next seven years. He was guilty of the sin of pride and was humbled so that he would realise "that the heavens do rule." (See Daniel chapter 4.)

Daniel interpreted the dream and told the king that he was the tree, and that he was to learn that though he ruled an empire there were yet far greater and more awesome powers which ruled in the heavenlies. We can read more about them in the New Testament. Paul, writing to the Ephesians explained our warfare, "against principalities against authorities, against the rulers of the darkness of this world, against wicked spirits in the heavenlies." (Eph.6:12.) In the same letter Paul also wrote that God has, "blessed us with all spiritual blessings in the heavenlies, in Christ." (1:3)

If our blessings are in the heavenlies and if there are watchers and holy ones keeping a look out on human affairs to prevent men from sinking in pride, committing what the Greeks called 'hubris'; there are also evil forces at work who also have their origins and their place in the heavenlies. Another verse in the same letter tells us that Satan is, "the prince of the power of the air." (2:2.) Again, writing to the Colossians Paul tells of two kingdoms, saying that, "the Father has…delivered us from the power of darkness translated us into the kingdom of His dear Son." (Col.1:13.)

It is clear in John chapter three that the Kingdom of God can only be entered by the New Birth. (vv.3.5,) This is where God rules and it is where His Word is paramount. On the other hand we also see that there is a kingdom run by the fallen hordes of Satan which is in opposition to all that is good and right and just.

To know more about this warfare we need to find out what the objectives of the participants are. God's purpose is to restore the world as it ought to have been and how it would have been before the fall. Indeed God does restore and He adds to this and, "restores that which He took not away". God adds extras to the things He does. (Mt.17:11.Ps.69:4.) Not only does He restore but He does new and better things. He allows us in this age to enter into the warfare which has been going on continually since the beginning of creation.

God, when we have finished up our brief spell in the front line then gives us rewards for good service. We have the chance to serve Him in a more elevated capacity in the New Age of Righteousness and as Paul wrote, "the time of my departure is at hand henceforth there is laid up for me a crown of righteousness…and for all them that love His appearing." (2Tim.4:6-8.)

The final victory is to be won by the Lord Jesus Christ alone. He defeated sin, death and Satan on the cross by Himself and He will return when His people's fortunes are at their lowest ebb. By the glory of His presence alone and by His Word He will defeat all the enemies of God and man and send them howling into the abyss and then into the Lake of Fire. Then after a thousand years of peace on this earth, and His judgment of the lawless, He will call into being a New Heavens and a New Earth.

Satan's purpose is also clear. Isaiah tells us about it as does Ezekiel. Isaiah wrote as follows concerning the ambition of Satan. "I will ascend into heaven. I will exalt my throne above the stars of God. I will sit also on the Mount of the Congregation in the sides of the north. I will ascend above the heights of the clouds. I will be like the Most High." (Is.14:13,14.) Of course this is madness but he had destroyed his reason in his madness, and in his pride. He probably still imagines he can reach this irrational goal. He certainly did when He approached the Lord Jesus in the wilderness offering Him "all the kingdoms of the world," and expecting the Lord to take the easy way out by giving homage to Satan and becoming his second in his administration. (Mt.4:8,9.)

It is quite possible that there were things hidden from him and possibly still are. Certainly one of the biggest targets for his attacks is the Deity of the Lord Jesus and the fact of the Godhead, three persons but one God. We do not have to understand it to believe it for God tells us it is so. In the very first sentence in the Bible we see the Trinity acting in unity since the subject, 'Elohim' (God), is plural and the verb 'created' is singular, 'He created'. We might think this to be bad grammar were it not that God had it written and He knows what He is saying.

So then, the Kingdom of God is where God Himself is the direct ruler. It is the sphere of His hegemony. Then the Kingdom of the Heavens must be where the heavens rule. However we have seen that this is where there is conflict. Rule was given to angels. We see angels looking after the destinies of nations. For instance, in Daniel chapters nine and ten we are introduced to angels who bring messages to the prophet. This is what angels are, they are messengers, that is what the word 'angel' means. (9:21. 10:5ff.)

We also find in chapter ten that there are other angels who are not on the same side as Daniel. They are referred to as "the prince of Persia" and "the prince of Greece" (10:12-14, 20,and 21) We find these have held up the angel messenger who was on his way with the answer to Daniel's prayers. This resulted in an intervention by another angel who is named as Michael, one of the chief princes. We meet him again in chapter twelve where he is revealed as, "the great prince which stands for the sons of thy people". (12:1.)

Here we see the heavenly conflict at its most bitter but we find even more angelic activity shown us in The Revelation. It is clear from this that the two Kingdoms are like two overlapping circles. Clearly those angels who come in response to Daniels prayers and the mighty angel who is the angel prince responsible for the nation of Israel are all part of God's Kingdom. The angels who have charge of the gentile nations, however, because of their opposition to the work of those of God, are part of Satan's kingdom.

The two Kingdoms are like two overlapping circles. There are things they have in common, but there are also significant differences. In the prophetic books we have a glimpse of the struggles going on in the heavenlies. The heavens rule but there is division and conflict and we take part in that conflict if we so wish and obey God's call for us to be His soldiers. We are recruited as Soldiers by the Lord Jesus. He is our Commanding Officer. (See2Tim.2:3,4.)

The Kingdom of God is different. We know that God rules directly over His Kingdom and that He is also an individual rule over each one of His subjects. We know about the preaching of the Gospel from the parable of the Sower and that we sow the seeds of God's Word broadcast as it were, scattering them over the fields. We see that the Lord Jesus is the supreme Sower and it is He who gives us His Word. Like Him we may fulfill the Psalm where it says. "He that goes forth weeping bearing seed for scattering, shall doubtless come again with rejoicing, bringing his sheaves with him." (Ps.126:6)

What goes on after that, in and with the true subjects of the Kingdom we cannot know, except for that which God is doing in and with us. Even then we do not know the how and the mechanisms He uses. It is, as Zechariah had explained to him. "Not by might, nor by power, but by My Spirit, says the Lord of Hosts." (Zech4:6.) How do we meet up with people with whom God wants us to speak? How do we learn the words and the Word? How is it that our feeble prayers are often so effective and how do we understand when God says "no!"

These are mysteries which we may be allowed to enter one day soon when at last we are with the Lord and will hear and learn many very wonderful things. Here is how God has explained it. "So is the Kingdom of God, as if a man should cast seed into the ground. And should sleep and rise night and day and the seed should spring and grow up, he knows not how. For the earth brings forth fruit of herself; first the blade, then the ear, after that the full corn in the ear, but when the fruit is brought forth, immediately He puts in the sickle because the harvest is come." It is the Lord's doing and it is marvelous in our eyes. (Mk.4:26.)

The Lord also mentions this mysterious time when the things closed to us are at work. He says in John chapter three. "The wind (Spirit) blows where it wishes, and you hear the sound thereof, but cannot tell whence it comes and whither it goes. So is everyone that is born of the Spirit." (Jn.3:8)

These parables must have been a mystery and a puzzle to those hearing Him. They were used to the common teaching that the

Kingdom of God was going to appear in great glory when the Gentile powers would be put down and Israel made the Head of the nations. They had good reason to think so. Did not both Isaiah and Micah foretell this time when Jerusalem should be the capital of the world? "And it shall come to pass in the last days that the mountain of the Lord's House shall be established in the top of the mountains, And shall be exalted above the hills. And all nations shall flow unto it. And many peoples shall go and say. 'Come and let us go up to the mountain of the Lord, to the House of the God of Jacob. And He will teach us of His ways, and we will walk in His paths.' For out of Zion shall go forth the Law and the Word of the Lord from Jerusalem. And He shall judger among the nations and shall rebuke many peoples And they shall beat their swords into plowshares, and their spears into pruning hooks. Nation shall not lift up sword against nation. Neither shall the learn war anymore." (Is.2:2-4. Mic.4:1-4)

At the time when the Lord Jesus takes the Kingdom then the two, the Kingdom of God and the Kingdom of the Heavens, are almost nearly overlapping. In the final state when God makes, "all things new" the two will be one and the same. First the "Kingdoms of this world are become the Kingdoms of our Lord and of His Christ. And He shall reign forever and ever." (Rev.21:5. 11:15.)

Unless we understand this situation we shall never be able to interpret the parables of the kingdom. We shall be in a fog of confusion and think of the parables as simple homilies given to make the Gospel clearer to little children. It is certainly a common confusion to assume that the Kingdom of God and the Kingdom of Heaven are one and the same thing.

Hearing they hear and do not understand.

The disciples asked Him the question. "Why speakest Thou to them in parables?" His answer was clear and was only given to the disciples and not made general knowledge to the crowds. Only the disciples were given the ability to understand. This is how He explained it. "Because it is given unto you to know the mysteries of the Kingdom of Heaven, but to them it is not given....Therefore speak I to them in parables; because they, seeing, see not, and hearing they hear not, neither do they understand." Mt.13: 11,13)

Neither the position, not the condition of Israel is understood by the theologians today any more than the Jewish theologians, in the days when these parables were spoken, understood their own Scriptures. They could not accept that the Kingdom was like seed growing in the ground with the harvest long months away. They did not understand the divide in time between the sowing and the harvest, nor the workings of the Kingdom of God during that time. Luke makes this clear. The Lord spoke the parable of the nobleman travelling into a 'far country' "because they thought that the kingdom of God was about to appear." (Luke 19:11)

Even yet they do not understand these things. Even though God is bringing them back to the land ready for that final persecution which will bring them to repentance and to "mourn for Him Whom they pierced," they do not realise what is ahead of them and what suffering they must endure.

The reality of the continual warfare going on between the forces of God and those of Satan, in and around this world is not really recognized by the theologians who profess to interpret parables as if they were to make things simple. Even if they do see that a conflict is in being they tend to see it as merely on a human level and do not care to recognise the cosmic and spiritual nature of our warfare.

The parable of the leaven is most often misunderstood; people see in it the eventual triumph of the Gospel as if our preaching were acting like leaven. In spite of passages in both Old and New Testaments to the contrary, showing that the leaven (yeast), in its working, is the way evil works in this world. Leaven is a symbol of corruption and of the corruption of evil at work at the present time, at work in this world, among people and nations and all human institutions.

The various levels of interpretation are also misunderstood. That the primary interpretation at the time and in a time yet future is about the nation of Israel quite clearly eludes many commentators. Sadly even some born again Christian commentators fail to understand this. All these interpret from their own stand point, so Christians only think in terms of the age now rapidly coming to a close, the age now present.

The cosmic conflict is still going on. It is in fact getting more fierce, more relentless and more cruel. We are privileged to live at this time but we need to gird ourselves in the armour which God has provided and which we neglect at our peril. Our enemies are immensely powerful and they are many. We are few but we do have the Spirit of the Living God in our hearts and on our side. Indeed The Lord Jesus, "is at our right hand that we should not be moved". (Ps.16:8)

What better way to end this introduction than with the words of Paul to the Ephesians. "Finally my brethren, be strong in the Lord and in the power of His might. Put on the whole armour of God that you may be able to stand against the wiles of the Devil....Wherefore take unto you the whole armour of God that you may be able to withstand in the evil day. And having done all, to stand. Stand therefore having your loins girt about with truth, and having on the breastplate of righteousness, and your feet shod with the preparation of the Gospel of peace. Above all taking the shield of faith wherewith you shall be able to quench all the fiery darts of the wicked. And take the helmet of salvation and the sword of the Spirit which is the Word of God." (Eph.6:1-17)

THE CROSS AND THE KINGDOM

The Kingdom

The Kingdom of God is entered by the new birth.(John 3:3,5.) One day soon it will be set up here on the earth. Daniel was told about this and a time scale given him. "Seventy weeks (i.e. 'sevens' of years=490 years) are determined upon thy people and upon thy holy city, to finish the transgression, and to make an end of sins, and to make reconciliation for iniquity, and to bring in everlasting righteousness and to seal up the vision and the prophecy and to anoint the Most holy (place)." (Dan.9:24. K.J.V. Newberry)

Subsequent verses make it clear that all this depends upon "Messiah the Prince," Who was to be "cut off" after the 69th week. This was clearly fulfilled at Calvary. The last, the seventieth week, awaits fulfillment, the church age having intervened. When the disciples asked, "Lord, wilt Thou, at this time restore again the kingdom to Israel," the Lord did not answer directly but told them that it was not for them to know the times and the seasons which the Father had kept under his own control.(Acts 1:6,7.)

During this age God, by means of the Gospel, calls out to the nations to repent. When the Lord finally sets His feet again on the Mount of Olives, then, and only then will evil be put down and Daniel's prophecy be fulfilled. (Zech.14:3,4 Acts1:10,11.)The Kingdom of God is now in people's hearts and minds. In that day to come it will be set up upon earth.

Riches and Power

One day soon God's people will be rich and will wield awesome authority. "Well done, thou good and faithful servant; thou hast been faithful over a few things I will make ruler over many things; enter thou into the joy of thy Lord." (Mt.25:21.)

This is not the age in which we live. Christians do not rule, nor should they rule. Paul rebuked the arrogance of the Corinthians saying, "ye have reigned as kings without us; and I would ye did reign, that we also might reign with you."(1Cor.4:8.) Clearly one day we shall reign but not in this age; but in the one to come.

The Present Age

The hymn aptly describes the attitudes of a world which is in rebellion against God and which hates our Lord Jesus Christ.

Our Lord is now rejected,

And by the world disowned.

By the Many still neglected,

And by the few enthroned.

And thus it will be until that glorious day when he returns in splendour with all his saints to bring in everlasting righteousness. This is the present age. The reason for the enigmatic answer by the Lord Jesus to the Disciple's question regarding the restoration of the Kingdom to Israel was that there was indeed a chance for Israel still to receive Him as Messiah. However He knew what was to be but they had to be given the chance.

The Acts is a Book of the transition between the offer of the Lord Jesus to Israel as their Anointed One and their rejection. So the stoning of Stephen at the end of Acts chapter seven sealed the rejection by Israel in the national capital. After that the Apostle to the Gentiles, Paul, is saved and raised up as an Apostle. The Gospel is also taken to the Gentiles for the first time in Caesarea by Peter and the Gospel also goes to Samaria and to Antioch.

27

Then the apostles are sent out all over the world. Paul in particular, as the Apostle to the nations, with his associates, takes the Gospel to the synagogue first then separates the gentile and Jewish converts into independent churches. Finally in chapter twenty eight we find Paul calling for the elders of the Jews in the Gentile capital, Rome, and telling them. "Be it known unto you therefore, that the salvation of God is sent to the nations, they will hear it." Having first quoted Isaiah six, verses nine and ten, (Acts 28:25-29)

This age then is an age of Grace with a door opened in heaven and the call of God for everyone to "come up hither" (Revelation4:1) Salvation is open to all who hear and obey god's call. And we are given and mission to take the gospel out to the world.

So, how should we then live? Christians share the rejection suffered by their Lord. They are despised as He was and their words are mocked as those of madmen or of drunkards. They have here, "no continuing city,"(Heb.13:14.) and they pass through this world rather than settle down in it. Indeed we are strangers and pilgrims, on our way to somewhere better, a city which has foundations whose builder and maker is God.(Heb.11:13. 1Pet 2:11. Heb.11:10, 16. 12:22.) Confirming this Paul wrote, "our citizenship is in heaven from whence also we look for the Saviour, the Lord Jesus Christ.(Phil 3:20. K.J.V. Newberry)

All this being so, first that we are to be like the Lord Jesus and, secondly, we are citizens of a foreign power, our loyalty is first and foremost to the Lord and to the Kingdom and the City which are His. Since we have eternal life then eternity matters more than time. Since we are pilgrims here, and strangers, we have no cause to value this world's goods nor its honours, nor its wealth for all these things are to pass away and only that which is laid up in heaven if of any lasting value and real worth.

"We are Ambassadors for Christ." (2Corinthians 5:20. Ephesians 6:20) Therefore we represent our King and our heavenly country to the people and the princes of this world. We speak of the peaceable attitude and message which God has toward the men of this age. We warn of the dangers to come. Whether they hear or whether they forbear. (Ezekiel 3:1-11. 33:1-17)

The Cross and Money

One might ask, are we then to give everything up in order to be Christians. The answer to that is "no!" for to become a Christian we turn to the Lord Jesus but at that moment we have to recognise that all that we have and are cannot procure our salvation. Only the work of Calvary can do that and only grace can bestow what we cannot earn, what we cannot buy and what we can never merit.

In that sense we have given everything up. That is our position as those who are saved and called, now, holy ones, saints of God. However God, though He could take us straight to heaven, in His wisdom does not. He leaves us here that we may serve Him and so lay up for ourselves treasure in heaven. We do this by becoming like the Lord Jesus in character in understanding and in wisdom. This is what God wants. This is what gives Him pleasure, to see us growing to be a little like His dear Son. (Rom.8:28,29).

Let us then not, "lay up for (ourselves) treasures upon earth, where moth and rust corrupt and where thieves break through and steal. But lay up for (ourselves) treasures in heaven where neither moth nor rust do corrupt and where thieves do not break through and steal for where (our) treasure is there will (our) heart be also. (Mt.6:19-21.)

Paul warns us that "the love of money is a root of all evil." (1Tim. 6:10) We have a guarantee from the Lord Himself that our needs will be supplied. (Phil 4:19) Bunyan gives us a graphic picture of this world's attractions in Vanity Fair which stood in the way of the Pilgrims in his *Pilgrim's Progress.* "Therefore at this fair are all such merchandise sold, as houses, lands, trades, places, honours, preferments, titles, countries, kingdoms, lusts, pleasures, and delights of all sorts..." Bunyan knew what it was to suffer for his love of the Lord Jesus Christ. He gives us a true picture of the worthlessness of what this world has to offer. To this John agrees. "Love not the world, neither the things that are in the world. If any man love the world, the love of the Father is not in him. For all that is in the world, the lust of the flesh and the lust of e eyes and the pride of life is not of the Father, but is of the world." (1Jn.2:15.)

Discipleship

When calling His disciples, the lord told them, "Follow Me!" (Mt 4:18,19) He also warned, "the foxes have holes and the birds of the air have nests but the Son of Man has not where to lay his head." (Mt. 8:20. Lk 9:58) We are no different from those Galilean fishermen the Lord called by the lake of that name. It is hard for us to cut our ties with the world and to cast ourselves adrift trusting that the Spirit of God will waft us where and how He will. We are creatures of earth and we find it a worrying step into the unknown to get up and to follow the "Man of Sorrows and Acquainted with Grief".

Discipleship is not about success in this world. It is not about position, promotion and status. It is not about money and possessions. It is about sorrow, suffering and being despised and patronised by the men and women of this world who will think we are fools.

Though Bible study is essential to true discipleship taking up the Cross is equally essential. Indeed it is what the Bible teaches and if we do not do it, we do not understand the Bible. The way of the Cross does not rest easily with advantage and promotion in this world. We should remember that it was the rulers of this world who actually crucified the Lord Jesus. Paul spoke and wrote, "the wisdom of God in a mystery." It was this "hidden wisdom which God pre-ordained before the ages unto our glory. Which none of the princes of this age knew, for had they known it they would not have crucified the Lord of Glory." (1Cor.2;6-8)

The Cross in the Lives of disciples

A rich young man came to the Lord Jesus and asked. "Good Master what shall I do, that I may inherit eternal life?" After telling him to obey the commandments, mentioning only those to do with other men, the young man argued that he had kept them from his youth. The Lord then told him. "One thing thou lackest, go thy way sell whatsoever thou hast, and give to the poor and thou shalt have treasure in heaven. And come, take up the cross and follow Me."(Mk10:17-22.cf Mt.19:16-22. Lk.18:18-23.)

The Lord explained how difficult it was for those with riches to enter the kingdom of God. So it was with that young man, he went away sorrowful. He could not face the challenge which discipleship brings. Perhaps that is why Paul explained to the Corinthians. "For ye see your calling brethren, how that not many wise men after the flesh, not many mighty, not many noble, are called. But God hath chosen the foolish things of the world to confound the wise. And God hath chosen the weak things of the world to confound the things which are mighty, and base things of the world and things which are despised, hath God chosen, and things which are not, to bring to nought the things which are. That no flesh should glory in his presence." (1Cor1:26-29)

We are not called to greatness but to weakness, to insignificance to harmlessness and to comparative poverty. Yet we do have security. No one may hurt us, no one may kill us, no one may rob us unless God gives them leave to do so. We are safe in His hands and when the time comes for us to leave for our home country then it will be at a time and in a manner of God's choosing.

Death and Triumph

The rich young ruler was told to take up the Cross. The Lord was inviting him to take up the means of his execution and rejection by this world. Satan and the world count us no more than a nuisance to be got rid of. They see us as parasites to be exterminated, and as embarrassments to be avoided and consigned to forgetfulness. A person who is carrying a cross is not coming back. He has said his goodbyes. He has no hopes for promotion in this world nor for success for he is about to be executed. He has no expectation for reprieve, for sentence has been passed and is about to be carried out. He is leaving this world and he is on a one way journey to the next world, and to a better one.

We are therefore counted as dead so we must not live as though this world was a comfortable place. We must not make ourselves comfortable for it is the abode and the kingdom of Satan. John told his readers that, "the whole world lies in the Wicked One (1Jn.5:19. K.J.V. Newberry) When the Devil offered "all the kingdoms of the World and the glory of them" to the Lord Jesus, he said, "for that is delivered unto Me and to whomsoever I will I give it." The Lord did not deny this; it is the state of this present evil age. (Mt.4:8-10. Mk 1:12,13. Lk.4:5-8) There could not be a clearer differentiation between the Kingdoms of this world and the Kingdom of God. We cannot sit on the fence; we must not, we cannot have both, we have to make a choice.

"A man's life consists not in the abundance of things he possesses." (Lk. 12:15) The Lord gave us yet another piece of advice. "He that find his life shall lose it; and he that loses his life for My sake shall find it. (Mt.10:39)

All Christians are "dead with Christ." We are dead to sin and, at the same time, we are risen with Him. (Rom. 6:7,8. 1Pet.2:24) Our "life is hid with Christ in God." (Col. 3:3.) To be alive with Christ we must be dead to the world as He has died and is risen again, so that, being dead, we "live with Him." (2Tim.2:11)

'Success' and betrayal

A meditation like this on the ways in which a Christian's life is altered by the reality of the cross makes any idea of compromise with the world anathema. The world betrayed and crucified its rightful king and has chosen to love its enemy rather than "The Son of God who loved us and gave Himself for us." (Gal. 2:20)

When we take up the cross daily we walk in His steps and plant our feet firmly in His footsteps. He is now crowned with victory crowns and with the diadems of power. We too shall be crowned with victor's crowns if we remain faithful. We too shall take authority under him and bear rule over cities and the farthest reaches of the universe. We too, who weep now, shall rejoice, for God Himself, "shall wipe away all ears from their eyes; and there shall be no more death, neither sorrow nor crying, neither shall there be any more pain..." (Rev.21:4)

Not yet for us to rule the world. But one day soon, under the Lord Jesus, we shall so do. For the present we may place our confidence in the Word of God and think about the words of Paul to Timothy. "But godliness with contentment is great gain for we brought nothing into this world and it is certain we can carry nothing out. And having food and covering let us be therewith content." (ITim.6: 6-8. K.J.V. Newberry)

What fools we are if we love the world and covet houses, lands and great possessions. What fools we are if we spurn our eternal reward for the passing pleasures of a decadent and corrupt age, what fools.

What fools we shall be if, at the end of it all we enter the presence of the Lord Jesus Christ with nothing, as if we have just been dragged out of a burning house which has consumed all that we owned, what fools. What fools we shall be to stand naked, watching all that we once held dear go up in smoke and in flames as worthless tinder and we stand amidst the charred ashes of burned wood, hay and stubble of a burned out wasted fruitless life, what fools.

All around us we shall see our dear brothers and sisters who have followed the Lord to Calvary, receive from His pierced hands their crowns of victory with a, "well done, good and faithful servant" from the Lord Himself. What fools we shall be to stand by while they are all confessed by name in the presence of God the Father while the Lord has nothing to say about us. (1Cor.3:11-15. Rev.3:5) "Saved! yet so as by fire." What fools!

THE PARABLE OF THE SOWER

A Parable, as has been rightly said, is something 'put alongside' to give a comparison. The word 'para' is the same as in parallel. By contrasting something familiar with something unfamiliar we may be able to understand the unfamiliar. However, in the Bible things are not always that simple. Sometimes the parable is designed not to be immediately apparent as to meaning. Sometimes they are actually designed to be obtuse, in order that people who bear ill-will against the Gospel message may not be able to understand.

They actually deal with matters that are mysteries. These are things which may only be revealed to the initiated. The theologians of the time were often antagonistic to the teachings of the Lord Jesus and that is given by him as a reason for hiding the meaning within a parable so that only disciples are able to unravel the interpretation. As has been explained above the experts then, just as the experts now, do not understand that the meaning and interpretation of these things may stretch out over many generations and God at various times deals in different ways. These parables show us some of the consistencies in the way God handles things whatever age we may be in.

When the disciples asked the Lord why He spoke in parables he replied that it was because people did not understand. He explained this in words which Paul also used with regard to the elders of the Jews in Rome. (Acts 28:25-29) "By hearing you shall hear and not understand. And seeing you shall see and shall not perceive. For this people's heart is waxed gross and their ears are dull of hearing and their eyes whey have closed lest at any time they should see with their eyes and hear with their ears and should understand with their heart and should be converted and I should heal them." (Is.6: 9,10. Mt.13: 14,15)

The point about the teaching of these parables is also that we are in the same condition. Even some born again Christians do not understand. The world certainly does not understand nor do the religious of Christendom. God is still at work, much of it in secret. He is preparing for that final day when the lord descends once more to the surface of this earth and all things will be put right; much to the shock and surprise of the majority of people and nations.

The Parable

'Behold' is an imperative. It tells us to take note or to pay strict and careful attention. Let us therefore pay careful and strict attention. Let us therefore picture in our mind a man in loose working clothes carrying a basket of seed or the seed in a fold of his garment over one arm while he scatters the seed in handfuls throwing it away from him across the broken earth. At times the farmer might put the seed in a sack with holes in it and carry it on the back of an ox so that the movement of the ox would allow the seed to fall in a more measured and regular pattern onto the ground. It also saved the sower having constantly to replenish his basket as the seed was used up; the ox being able to carry a much heavier weight of seed. More simply it has to be remembered that not all men who till the earth are able to afford help. They have to make do with the efforts of their own hands and arms.

Up and down the field they go, the seed being scattered into the ground though some, as the parable states does get taken or fails to germinate. A path runs alongside the field and the birds, knowing full well that a man behaving in this way probably denotes food, will be already hovering or flying in readiness to swoop down and scoop up the food, left them by human hands, in their beaks.

When the seed falls on the ploughed and broken earth it drops into the small gaps between the clods, and there starts the slow but steady process of germination. That also depends on sun and rain but these are out of the man's competence, he must rely on God and the elements in the hope of a harvest to come.

As with all tillage stones constantly rise to the surface from the subsoil below. These are picked up by the men and taken to the edges of the field. They may be used to fill up potholes in the roadway, or they may be added to the piles of stones at the corners of the field which mark its boundaries.

Also between the path and the field there may be border of mixed stones and weeds. There may be as well a similar weedy border between fields. Sometimes the thorns and thistles grow around the base of trees where these grow. Some scattered seeds only find a place among the stones of in the soil where they grow with the weeds which are probably already well established. In both cases the seedlings either are burned up and withered by the sun or choked by the rank growth of the weeds.

There are different personalities and different kinds of environments and not all seed falls on good ground where there is a ready acceptance of the Word of God. The gap between seedtime and harvest is implicit here as it is more clearly explained in the parable in Mark chapter four. There days and nights go by and it is stressed that the process of germination in the earth and then the mystery of the growth of the plant to full stature and of the formation of corn in the ears is only alluded to and cannot be explained for it is hidden from human eyes. (Mk.4:26-29)

This, as has already been suggested, must have caused some problems for the Jews who were expecting the appearance of Messiah and a Swift establishment of God's kingdom. Many were

37

expecting something to happen. More than a few had suspicions that the Lord Jesus was indeed the promised Messiah who would do all this. However doubts must have arisen as He told them all these things. Nevertheless it was necessary, for Israel rejected Him whom God had sent. Two long millennia soon set in while the Jews wandered, without a home, and are only just returning to their homeland. There they are to be brought under the justice and discipline of God which will eventually lead to their repentance, to the return of the Lord Jesus and His establishing of His Kingdom upon the earth.

As far as we are concerned it is necessary for us to empty our minds of traditional and pre-conceived ideas. Traditional teaching has a parable as something literally 'thrown alongside' in order that people, especially children should be able to understand. Even where there is an understanding of the position of Israel in Bible prophecy, grotesque interpretations are still evident.

The actual mode of teaching employed by the Lord Jesus is also foreign to us. We are used to hundreds and more of years of men standing in front of a congregation or even mounted in a pulpit to harangue the faithful. The whole manner of the gathering of people to hear the Lord by the lakeside was very informal. Indeed I have said 'to hear' the Lord Jesus.

Of course people did listen and He did, from time to time, give a rather more lengthy discourse. However we note how He broke off for a private talk with the disciples from time to time. This suggests that the Lord may even have walked among the crowds sat on the ground and listened to questions from individuals and small groups.

The seven parables we have here would not have taken long to speak. Clearly He either told others as well or there was plenty of informal discussion as I have already suggested. The formal lecture, usually referred to as a sermon is an inefficient and clumsy mode of teaching and observation of such and its results shows that very little learning is in fact achieved. I would suggest that more dialogue, more questioning by learners and less lecturing by 'teachers' should take place.

People, men in particular, who go on the Christian lecture circuits actually achieve very little. If therefore the hearers do not learn then the whole thing must have been an exercise in the blowing of hot air. The most important thing to teach the young is that they should be able to search out things for themselves. The Bereans are a prime case in point. They clearly listened to what the Apostle Paul had to say, for they, "received the Word with all readiness of mind". But it did not end there. Even though they had heard from the Apostle himself this would not do; it was not enough. The natural consequence was that they "searched the Scriptures daily whether these things were so". (Acts 17:10) Because of this twofold keenness to receive and to check up they have been noted as "more noble". Would that all God's people were so. Would that God's people did more questioning, more searching and more dialogue. And less bland acceptance of the words and ideas of preachers.

If this all day meeting by the Sea of Galilee was carried on in the informal way suggested by the text then we would do well to follow the example given us by the Lord Jesus Himself, then confirmed for us by the Apostles Paul and Peter. Church elders, wrote Peter, are to be shepherds who "feed the flock of God." Paul also pointed this out to the elders of the church at Ephesus when he called them to him to Miletus during his journey to Rome. (Acts 20:17) He said to them, "Take heed therefore unto yourselves, and to all the flock over the which the Holy Spirit has made you overseers, to feed the church of God, which He has purchased with

His own blood." (Acts 20:28.) 'Overseers' here is the word often wrongly translated 'bishops' while 'feed' means to "feed as shepherds" or 'pastors'. We see from this that the churches in the first century had several overseers and that these were also pastors. These would have been engaged in a teaching ministry almost daily, following Paul's example where again he reminded the Ephesian elders, "I kept back nothing that was profitable unto you but have showed you and have taught you publicly and from house to house." How many church elders I wonder follow this example today. There are some of course but they are not in the majority. Where there is just one minister, or pastor, then he can hardly be expected to visit regularly, for teaching purposes, the whole of the flock of God.

Consider the Proverb (20:5.) Counsel in the heart of man is like deep water. But a man of understanding shall draw it out." People through the ages are often inarticulate. They are regarded as ignorant and dull by the ruling classes, even as foolish and incapable of being educated. This is not what the Bible tells us and it is not what History demonstrates. Paul, wrote to the Corinthians explaining how God worked with the Common people. "For you see your calling brethren, how that not many wise men after the flesh, not many mighty, not many noble are called; But God has chosen the foolish things of the world to confound the wise and God has chosen the weak things of the world to confound the things which are mighty and base things of the world and things which are despised has God chosen and things which are not to bring to nought the things that are. That no flesh should glory in His presence." (1Co.1:26-29)

People do not have to remain in this state. Our fore-fathers in Britain set up ragged and charity schools and in the other English speaking countries too. They did this because it was right to do so. Though they hoped that people would convert to Christianity through the teaching they received, they also believed that children and grown-ups ought to be able to read for themselves. They did not consider that folk should be left to have their minds filled with the superstitious nonsense of priests and of political demagogues. Christians believed then and believe now that people ought to be able to learn, and to learn independently and so to think for themselves.

Christians all over the world run schools which take in people of all religions and none. They do not succeed in helping all but a few to become Christians but they believe that the young people they teach are better for a liberal and open education which enables them to be Bereans and to think for themselves.

Jonathan Rose in his *The Intellectual Life of the British Working Class* shows that for over two centuries many working people in Britain raised themselves up by their bootstraps by banding together in clubs and paying in a very small amount of copper out of their wages to purchase books which they then shared. The result was a literate, questioning and argumentative working class.

One of the supreme examples of this is the Medical Missionary and explorer, David Livingstone, who worked in a cotton mill, reading while working and attending University at night to gain his medical qualification. He is an example to us all. Would that we gave this sort of determination and concentration, as did Livingstone, today. Paul, writing to Timothy encouraged with the words. "Study (give diligence) to show yourself approved unto God, a workman that needs not to be ashamed, rightly dividing the Word of Truth." (2Timothy2:15) We must ask ourselves what it means to "rightly divide the Word of Truth?"

Now we have state schools which more or less follow a curriculum laid down by the government with the implicit and explicit materialistic aims of government not so carefully concealed. There is only poor moral education and little moral example. Indeed there cannot be for materialism has no morality and post modernism encourages everyone to form their own values based on expediency, or to accept the values cobbled together by the ruling political classes.

Moreover the prevailing Darwinist natural selection gives us survival as the supreme value. Consequently we have a violent, aggressive and course population with every man doing that which is right in his own eyes. It is a population suspicious, aggressive and sly with every man's hand against that of his fellows.

The Lord did not give a sustained several hour long lecture with a break for lunch. Nor did He use the boat as a pulpit. The boat served to separate Him from the people. This also served to demonstrate the moral separation which was also in evidence. The Lord's informal breaks for talk with His disciples tells us that they, or even He, from time to time may have moved among the crowds. However that is speculation. What is stressed is that He spoke in parables because as He explained to the disciples the reasons for speaking to the crowd in parables. "Because it is given unto you to know the mysteries of the Kingdom of the Heavens but to them it is not given. For whosoever has to him shall be given and he shall have more abundance....Therefore I speak to them in parables because they seeing see not and hearing they hear not, neither do they understand. (Mt.13: 11-17)

A pattern and a purpose

We might ask why the Lord did not go among them and explain, perhaps He did. However to understand this we must go back to the previous chapter and see how the leaders and teachers of the Jews were already banded together in order "to destroy Him".

(Mt.12: 1) The following verses in chapter twelve show how, in spite of His healing miracles, the Pharisees argued that He did these things by the power of Satan, thus committing the sin against the Holy Spirit. (v24, 31,32)

The Lord was referring to a principle stated by Moses when He said that these things were revealed to disciples. Moses wrote. "The secret things belong unto the Lord our God. But those things which are revealed belong unto us and to our children for ever, that we may do all the words of this Law." (Deut.29: 29)

Following this same example, after the telling of the parable of the Sower and then explaining matters to the disciples, he told the parable of the Tares in the Field and then those of the Mustard Seed and the Leaven. After that He sent the crowds away and went into 'the house'. There he interpreted the parable of the Tares in the Field but to the disciples only.

In these interpretations we are given the ways in which the Lord showed the symbolism. Scripture must interpret Scripture as Peter taught. (2Pe.1: 20,21) The verses 36-43 give us confirmation of what we may have concluded with regard to the Parable of the Sower. The Lord Himself is He who sows the seed. However in the case of the Tares the seeds are either good Christian people from the Lord or evil people sown by Satan. The field itself is the world and this helps us to understand the Sower.

Equally the birds are agents of the 'Wicked One' so we may understand that generally wherever we come across birds in Scripture, they often represent the demonic forces of Satan. Interestingly enough there are birds who make themselves at home in the branches of the great tree in Daniel where the tree is Nebuchadnezzar the ruler of the Babylonian empire. (Dan4:10-12.) We see here, from the wider context, how Satan uses his agents to spread his rule among the nations and empires of this world and so how He will do so in the final world empire of the last days before the Lord returns to the earth. He takes over the administration of the systems of government, even of educational systems which may even have been founded by Christian people. He also takes the precious seed of the Word of God from the hearts of the ignorant and hard hearted individuals lest it find a rest there and germinates and brings forth fruit for God.

Paul writes to the Corinthians explaining how this subversion goes on. He says that he, the Devil, "blinds the minds of them which believe not, lest the light of the glorious Gospel of Christ, Who is the image of God, should shine unto them." (2Cor.4: 3,4)

The stony ground too is not the place for seedlings to flourish. With a rain shower they may germinate but they soon dry up and shrivel and die in the heat of the sun. The Lord likens this to troubles and persecutions. There was no deep root in the personality therefore no strength of character. The conversion, if one may call it that is weak and only superficial. How often this happens. There are plenty of nice, respectable people who cannot take hardship, whether it is physical, emotional of mental. They stay nice people but their attendance at Bible study or prayer meeting ceases. This is followed by increased absence from the Breaking of Bread until they relapse back into the world. These will be the sort of people who succumb when the Final world Emperor orders that all people should have his mark and not to do so will mean that people who refuse will not be able to buy nor to sell.

We ought not to judge these dear people of course. We are in no position to do so. We cannot do what God does and look on the hearts; we only see the outward appearance and behaviour, not the true state of the heart. (1Sam.6:7) The state of the heart is shown to decline with sloth or with self-will. We can all get lazy and neglect our spiritual exercise of reading, of praying and of witnessing.

In Malachi's day there were those who were saying it was a waste of time to serve God. "Your words have been stout against Me says the Lord. Yet you say, 'what have we spoken against thee'. You have said, 'it is vain to serve God' and 'what profit is it that we have kept His ordinance?'" (Mal.1: 13,14) Let us not say that we today are not also guilty of thinking, speaking and acting like this.

We may read elsewhere of stony hearts. Ezekiel foretold the rebirth of Israel under the power and grace of God. "And I will take the stony heart out of their flesh and will give them an heart of flesh, that they may walk in My statutes and keep My ordinances and do them." (Ez.11: 19) Though this speaks primarily concerning Israel, it also states a fixed and general principle in God's dealings with individuals in this age as well as with the Nation which is His. In John chapter three the Lord Jesus told Nicodemus about being born again. (Jn.3:5-8) He did not understand. He too was ignorant, though as a rabbi he ought to have understood the prophecy of Ezekiel already quoted and a further one where the whole process is even more clearly stated. "A new heart also will I give you, and a new spirit will I put within you. And I will take away the stony heart out of your flesh and give you an heart of flesh. And I will put My Spirit within you." (Ez.36: 26,27)

This seems to suggest that it is all of God's doing and that there is no room for man's free will in all of it. If that were so then the period of the Great Tribulation would have been wasted. It is probable that the very words of Isaiah chapter fifty-three are those which Israel will speak when they finally mourn for Him whom they pierced. (See Zech.12:10-14)

Consider the following facts. In the above passage they mourn. These are not crocodile tears they shed. Having had poured out upon them the Spirit of grace and of supplications, they mourn. They could have hardened their hearts but they do not. It is their choice. It is a choice that the remnant of Israel will make one wonderful day in the future but perhaps very soon. In Isaiah, though it does not say they make a free choice the language is that of choice. "Surely He has borne our griefs and carried our sorrows, but we did esteem Him stricken, smitten of God and afflicted. But He was wounded for our transgressions; He was bruised for our iniquities. The chastisement of our peace was upon him and with His stripes we are healed. All we like sheep have gone astray; we have turned every one to his own way; and the Lord has laid on Him the iniquity of us all." (Is 53:3-6ff) This is the moment as in Psalm 73 where the Psalmist suddenly finds and understands the answer to all his problems concerning the success and prosperity of the wicked as he enters the sanctuary of God and sees things from God's point of view. (Vv.16,17)

We must remember that these parables were spoken first to Jews. However simple it may seem to supposedly Christian people or people who have been brought up in a Judeo-Christian based culture, it would have presented serious difficulties for the Jewish hearers. We understand from John chapter three how Nicodemus failed to grasp what may seem to us obvious. "How can these things be?" was his worried response. The Lord, with a loving rebuke asked him gently. "Are you a teacher of Israel and you do not know these things." He should have known but failed to make the connection.

If the side of the pathway, the pathway itself and the stony ground at the edges of the field were unfruitful having no way for seed to take proper root nor be hidden from the ever-hungry birds then the unweeded patches in the corners of the field or round the bases of any trees also made the survival of young plants doubtful.

Thorns and thistles are the result of the curse where Adam could only eat by the sweat of his brow. (Gen.3:17-19) Things changed and man was condemned to work for a living. Nevertheless this was also a blessing for work gives a person an identity. Work can also give a person dignity, or it should do if work, as it should be, were dignified. Sadly a lot of work which people are condemned to do is degrading as well as poorly paid and tedious.

In the parable, the thorns and thistles are likened to, "the cares of this world and the deceitfulness of riches". (v.22) Interestingly it is the man who does physical labour who gains most from the 'sweat of his brow'; the rich man has an uneasy and troubled existence. "The sleep of a laboring man is sweet, whether he eat little or much. But the abundance of the rich will not suffer him to sleep." (Ecc.5:12) What a contrast this is and yet men still strive to be wealthy and powerful, what folly."

The man or woman "whose God is the Lord," has no such difficulties. He has the promise from God Himself through the Apostle. "My God shall supply all your need according to His riches in glory by Christ Jesus." (Phil.4:1) We also have the assurance from Matthew's Gospel. "Take no thought for your life what you shall eat or what you shall drink, nor yet for the body what you shall put on. Is not the life more than food and the body more than clothing?" (Mt.6:25)

With regard to riches, having the assurance that God will always supply all we need then we can give ourselves to amassing the true wealth in the only place where it matters. "Lay not up for yourselves treasures upon earth where moth and rust corrupt and where thieves break through and steal. But lay up for yourselves treasures in heaven where neither moth nor rust corrupt and where thieves do not break through nor steal. For where your treasure is there will your heart be also." (6:19-21)

This is (above) how to be good ground but we all have that choice. If we let the cares and the troubles worry us then we become fruitless. But do we have to do this. The answer must be "no!" Since we are given the exhortation to humble ourselves it is human nature to act as if we know better. 'Humbling' ourselves is not something the man of the world takes to kindly. However the Word of God is sure. "Humble yourselves therefore under the mighty hand of God that He may exalt you in due time. Casting all your care upon Him, for He cares for you." (1Pe.5: 6,7)

The pride of man is such that we resent having to obey. Yet there is no shame, indeed there is great dignity in obeying God. Slothfulness is also another way in which we let cares and the deceits of the things the world to undermine our Christian life and witness. Consider what the Proverb says is the result of laziness and then let us consider our own failings. "I went by the field of the slothful and by the vineyard of the man void of understanding. And lo, it was all grown over with thorns, and nettles had covered the face thereof. And the stone wall thereof was broken down." (Prov.24: 30,31)

We see therefore, that it is possible to make ourselves and take control of ourselves. To form our own characters and so to become 'good ground'. That is to conform ourselves to be like the Lord Jesus. That Christ may be formed in us. (Gal.4:19) God then controls all our circumstances in order that this comes about. "And we know that all things work together for good to them that love God to them who are the called according to His purpose. For whom He did foreknow, He also did predestinate to be conformed to the image of His Son, that He might be the firstborn among many brethren. Moreover whom He did predestinate, them He also called and whom He called them He also justified and whom He justified them He also glorified." (Rom.8:28-30)

God, of course, already knows who will obey Him and to what degree of obedience they will attain. Because He knows who will listen to the Gospel and who will respond, those who He knows already he predestinates to be like the lord Jesus. However the level of likeness we attain to is according to how much we obey Him. He disciplines us and guides us but we are still human beings with free will and we make the decisions at each step to go one step further. Indeed we are so led by the Spirit of God that only if we are willing do we see the next step. "If any man wills (determines) to do His (God's) will, he shall know of the teaching." (Jn7:17)

In another place we see that, as God's sons, He disciplines us and as we accept that correction so we learn and we grow. "For whom the Lord loves He chastens and scourges every son whom He receives. If you endure chastening, God deals with you as with sons. For what son is he whom the father chastens not. But if you be without chastisement, whereof all are partakers then are you bastards and not sons." (Heb.12:5-8)

With regard to the actual characteristics which God wants to see formed in us we only have to go to the so called, 'sermon on the mount', or perhaps to the shorter version which tells us the fruit of the Spirit which all 'good ground' brings forth. "But the fruit of the Spirit is love, joy, peace, longsuffering, gentleness, faith, meekness, self-control. Against such there is no law." (Gal.5: 22,23)

This is not a tick list on some celestial clipboard. We may all have a measure of these virtues at some of the time to some degree or another. We may not judge one another as to our spiritual state of growth. It is too complex. Only God can do that so we must leave it to Him Who sees into our deepest thoughts and intentions. As we grow more and more Christ-like we shall be less and less concerned with our own progress and more and more concerned to help others to prosper spiritually. That is another quality we should seek to emulate for was not the Lord Jesus the "Chief Shepherd of the sheep?" And ought we not take on, as we mature, a pastoral role encouraging and teaching and going alongside to help and to heal?(1Pe.5:1-4)

THE PARABLE OF THE TARES

"The Kingdom of Heaven is likened to a man who sowed good seed in his field. But while men slept his enemy came and sowed tares among the wheat." (Mt.13: 24,25)

Having explained the meaning of the parable of the Sower, at its simplest, the Lord went on to tell this parable. Though that of the Sower is simple and its meaning clear; this parable is more complex and takes us from that present time, by implication back into the past, and certainly on to the future and the judgment.

There is also the time between these when the disciples ask the reason for the parables. However, though He did not say who the Sower was in the interpretation of that parable it was possibly because it was obvious and inevitable with sowing broadcast. Anyway it was simply an introduction which set the scene for the other parables. He was explicit, however when He came to explain this second parable to the disciples.

Because the parable of the Sower showed some general principles of sowing the Word of God it is then also clear that anyone can sow this provided they are chosen to do so. That is if they are true born again Christians. The second parable is more explicit and deals with serious problems to do with the Kingdom of Heaven and the Kingdom of God.

"He that sows the good seed is the Son of Man, and the field is the world. The good seed are the children of the Kingdom. But the tares are the children of the Wicked One, and the Enemy that sowed them is the Devil. The harvest is the final end of the age and the reapers are the angels." (vv37-39)

Whereas the first parable simply has an agricultural theme this goes far beyond the day to day life of the rural community. It is to do with the heavenly, the spiritual and the eternal. It takes us out of this mundane existence and leads us into the cosmic battleground where we are called on to, "put on the whole armour of God" (Eph.6: 10-13)

To begin it will be useful for us to know the meaning of the title 'Son of Man'. It occurs about ninety times in the prophecy of Ezekiel and eighty in the Gospels. Any title or name has a meaning and a significance. The first occurrence of that title or name may give us its significance. In this case we must first ask why Ezekiel was called 'Son of Adam'. In chapter two of Ezekiel we see that the race of Adam is a sinful and rebellious people. Not surprisingly Israel who we would have expected to be the best of the race have also, by the time of the prophet, also turned out to be a sinful people. God said to Ezekiel. "Son of Man (Adam), I send thee to the children of Israel, to a rebellious nation that have rebelled against Me. And their fathers have transgressed against Me, even unto this day" (2:3)

In this, as Son of Man, Ezekiel is both a representative of the human race and a picture of the Lord Jesus Who came to His own (things) and His own (people) received Him not. The prophet is also a demonstration of how any of us may, by being both descended from Adam and being "born of God" be God's representatives to this evil world and, by being so, we also become like the Lord Jesus.

Ever since Adam disobeyed God the inhabitants of the world have been sinful. It is part of our character which we inherit from Adam. There is a fault in our genetic make-up brought about by that separation from God, the source of life, when Adam disobeyed. If it is true of the race as a whole then it is particularly true of Israel, who once answered God. "All that the Lord has spoken we will do." These words were then relayed to God by Moses. (Deut.5:27)

Almost as soon as they had said this they were dancing naked before an idol entirely forgetful of Moses and the God who had delivered them from slavery in Egypt.

God then gave them the sacred trust of His Law. Of course they could not keep the law though some, especially the religious men of the first century, even imagined that they were close to it even actually of achieving it. In fact they had always been a rebellious people. They are our example. If Israel could not keep the law then we certainly cannot. "Now we know that whatsoever the Law says it says to them who are under the Law. That every mouth may be stopped and all the world become guilty before God."

So Ezekiel became a representative of the human race before God. He was given a vision of God and God called him the 'Son of Adam'. He was a Jew but not living in the land of Israel but in Babylonia among the nations. He thus is a symbolic representative of the whole race and to the whole race. Not only is he called 'Son of Adam in the beginning of the prophecy but he is also given the title at the end when he sees the new temple and the millennial state. (47:6) This tells us also that the Lord Jesus, the true and ultimate 'Son of Man' is at the beginning and at the end of all things.

In the same way the Lord Jesus is God's representative. He is however also God the Son who becomes the Son of Adam. This is how His line is traced back, to Adam then to God in the Genealogy in Luke's Gospel. (Lk.3:38) The Lord was what no ordinary human descended from Adam could ever be but was that one being who in His own person could embrace both heaven and earth, bring the two together and reconcile us to God (Job 9:33). As Ezekiel saw the healing waters flowing out from God's temple so the Lord Jesus Himself it is, Who sends those healing waters. He alone, it must be, who causes the desert to blossom and the barren ground to bring forth greenery and all the world to rejoice.

This parable tells us about these ages from the creation to the flood and from the flood to the coming of the Lord Jesus and then to this present time and on into the rule of Messiah for one thousand years. He it is who is 'the Son of Adam'; He Who sows the good seed who are the 'children of the kingdom'. Alas there is still the work of the Evil One who is still allowed to carry on his destructive and subversive activity. He also sows and sees to it that his children are there among the 'children (sons) of the Kingdom.

There are parallels with the Parable of the Mustard Seed. Whereas the birds lodging in the branches are demonic beings who take over and use that which was planted by God so there are servants of Satan who are found among the people of God and who look very much like them. We are being warned about these, but do we heed the warning?

The other parable that of the leaven is also similar. The demonic beings, their human instruments and the false teachings and corrupt living they represent show us in three simple illustrations the way things happen in this world and the strategies of the powers of the Evil One.

This is not surprising. Paul in his second letter to the Corinthians, wrote. "For such are false apostles, deceitful workers, transforming themselves into the apostles of Christ. And no marvel for Satan himself is transformed into an angel of light. Therefore it is no great thing if his ministers also be transformed as the ministers of righteousness, whose end shall be according to their works." (2Cor.11: 13,14) The Lord Jesus had already said something very similar. He warned of those who come in disguise. "Beware of false prophets which come to you in sheep's clothing, but inwardly they are ravening wolves. You shall know them by their fruits." (Mt.7: 15,16)

These are 'the children of the Devil'. They are religious, they have a form of Godliness but their hearts are far from Him. "You are of your father the Devil," said the Lord Jesus to his enemies who cast aspersions on his birth and on his mother. He continued: "And the lusts of your father you will do. He was a murderer from the beginning and abode not in the truth, because there is no truth in him. When he speaks a lie, he speaks of his own for he is a liar and the father of it." (Jn. 8:44,45)

In this parable we are told that He sowed seed in His field. He is the rightful ruler of this world though Satan for the time being has a brief freedom to do as he pleases, within the limits set by God. In this way Satan, "while men slept," sows confusion among the people of God and throughout the world.

"He that keeps thee will not slumber. Behold He that keeps Israel shall neither slumber nor sleep." (Ps. 121:3,4) God does not sleep. It is, "while men slept". We see this often and there are frequent times when we ought to be watchful but our attention wanders, we drowse and fall into a deep sleep. By contrast Scripture warns us to be wakeful. "Therefore let us not sleep as do others, but let us watch and be sober. For they that sleep, sleep in the night and they that be drunken are drunken in the night. But let us who are of the day be sober,..." (1Thess 5:6,7)

The true character of the darnel (tares) is that its seeds, unlike wheat, to which it is similar in appearance, are poisonous to man and to many domestic animals. These men and women who make a show of theology and who seek to be leaders among Christian people are deadly and full of poison. I have seen keen young Christians, thinking they are going to prepare for God's service, choose a university or college course in theology. Almost without

55

exception these young people are subverted by the University and College teachers who themselves do not believe the Bible and who persuade their students that they do not have to do so either.

These young people often, when they have graduated, become clerics and, in so doing become as bad as their teachers; blind leaders of the blind also. The Pharisees had plenty of wranglings and disputings but as the Lord accused them. "Woe unto you scribes and Pharisees, hypocrites! For you shut up the Kingdom of Heaven against men. For you neither go in yourselves nor suffer them that are entering to go in....Ye compass sea and land to make one proselyte, and when he is made you make him two fold more the son of Hell (Gehenna) than yourselves. Woe unto you blind guides..." (Mt.23:13-16) The Lord Jesus spoke a lot about blindness and blind people. He said that the Pharisees were, "blind leaders of the blind". (Mt.15:14)

In the Revelation and in chapters two and three we have warnings addressed to the churches by the Lord Jesus Himself. It is a pity we do not read these and take them to heart. The start of all the trouble is as the Lord accused the church at Ephesus. "I have somewhat against thee because thou hast left thy first love." (Revelation2:4) After that we read of tares among the wheat. Though the Ephesians hated the deeds of the Nicolaitanes, the people conquerors, these showed themselves busy teaching in the church at Pergamos, which also followed their teaching. (2:6, 15.16)

There are other examples of tares among the wheat. In Smyrna for instance there where those who claimed to be Jews but who were the 'synagogue of Satan. In Pergamos there were also those who held the doctrine of Balaam who, unable to turn God from His people managed to turn God's people against God. Jezebel taught the church at Thyatira to commit sacrilege and to worship idols and

56

again at Philadelphia there were Judaizing tendencies which the Lord condemned. (Rev.2: 6,9,15, 20ff. 3:9)

People love religion and there is in all our hearts a tendency towards legalism. By this tendency we want to make other people do what we think is right or what we think the Bible teaches. We fail to understand and to recognise our own weaknesses and prejudices. It is often a question of the mote and the beam. (Mt.7:5) We fail to see and understand clearly other people's prejudices because of our own.

The New Testament shows us local churches which are led by the local elders. These, "feed the flock of God,… taking oversight thereof, not by constraint, but willingly, not for filthy lucre, but of a ready mind, neither as being lords over God's heritage but being examples to the flock. And when the chief Shepherd shall appear, (they) shall receive a crown of glory that fades not away." (1Pe.5:1-4)

This ought to be clear enough to anyone. Sadly everything which Peter warned about was soon being put in place so that by the end of the second century or even earlier we had 'bishops' who were either over one church or over a group of churches. Such is human nature. Such is the process of institutionalisation which inevitably happens whenever anything is left in human hands.

To show how the writers in the New Testament were in agreement about this we only have to scan the writings of Paul and those of John. In Acts twenty Luke records how Paul called the elders of the church of Ephesus to meet him in Miletus where he gave then a series of gravely serious warnings. Here is what he said as Luke wrote it down for us.

"Take heed therefore unto yourselves, and to all the flock over which the Holy Spirit has made you overseers, to feed the church of God which he purchased with his own blood. For I know this, that after my departing shall grievous wolves enter in among you, not sparing the flock. Also of you own selves shall men arise speaking perverse things to draw away disciples after them. Therefore watch and remember that by the space of three years I ceased not to warn every one night and day with tears." (Acts 20:28-31)

The very thing Peter warned about is often but not always the reason men and women follow a way which shows them to be set where they are because they are the Devil's children. As Balaam was willing to be hired by Balak to curse Israel so many, but not all, follow "the way of Balaam son of Bosor who loved the wages of unrighteousness." (2Peter 3: 3-7)

Jude compares these false Christians to those who "go in the way of Cain". That is they love to offer to God their own worthlessness and the worthless works of their own hands. Clerics see themselves as the conscience of the nation. They so are puffed up with their own self-righteousness that they forget that the only Righteous One was the Lord Jesus. They also follow the "gainsaying of Korah". That is they are in denial of those who are better than themselves or have been given a different task to perform of which they are jealous. (Jude 11, Numbers 16)

Korah and his companion were envious of the status God had given to Moses and to Aaron. Though Korah was a Levite and so had an important task to perform in the precincts of the Tabernacle and with the vessels of the Tabernacle when the tribes were on the move He still wanted the priesthood. For this he perished.

So it is that men see that being an academic or being a cleric gives status and an easy life. They are then puffed up with the qualifications they must need obtain in order to achieve the status they covet.

This ambition in its basic naked striving for dominance is revealed to us by John. He speaks of a man called Diotrephes, "who loves to have the pre-eminence". Here at its crudest is the nature of the bully who will often grovel to someone more powerful than he is but who loves to intimidate, control or manipulate those who appear to be weaker than himself. In this case he denied John the Apostle access to the church. We have these sort of people, Cains, Balaams, Korahs, and a Diotrephes, in every walk of life. They strut and posture or they lie in wait behind the scenes controlling with a word here, a remark there, the things other people think, do or say. It does not matter whether it be good or evil. What matters is that these weak and empty cowards, have control, not self-control, for that is the most difficult of all but control over others.

That this has always gone on, that it is part of human nature to want either to dominate or to submit, is shown by Jeremiah who complained about the religious leaders in his day, saying. "A wonderful and horrible thing is committed in the land. The prophets prophesy falsely and the priests bear rule by their means. And my people love to have it so. And what will you do in the end thereof." (Jer. 5:30,31)

Peter the Apostle could almost have had this passage among those in his mind when he wrote the following. "But there were false prophets also among the people, even as there shall be false teachers among you who privately shall bring in destructive heresies, even denying the Lord that bought them and bring upon themselves swift destruction. And many shall follow their pernicious ways, by reason of whom the way of truth shall be evil spoken of. And through covetousness shall they with feigned words make merchandise of you…" (2Pe.2:1-3) The word 'pernicious' is again as in a previous sentence a word which means 'destructive'. That is precisely what false teachers do. So where there is division, where there is confusion and where there is assertive argument among Christians we may well also find the human tares.

More recently Erich Fromm in his work *The Fear of Freedom*, comments on this phenomenon where there is a drive to dominate and at the same time a drive to submit. It seems that many of us have a fear of the crowd and yet we also fear not being part of it and so tend to take on the ideas and opinions of those around us. Independent Christian thinkers are few and far between. We all echo the opinions of the leaders of our denomination or of our educators and fear to challenge them.

The proverb counsels us regarding the way of true Christian virtue. It is not to control others but to know ourselves and to have control over our evil passions and to be able to direct our minds and our hearts and so our bodies to what is good, kind and regardless of self. "He that is slow to anger is better than the mighty; and he that rules his own spirit than he that takes a city." (Prov,16:32)

The greatest freedom is often to force ourselves to do what is right and good rather than to give in to our passions and do what pleases our lower nature. "Let us consider one another to provoke unto love and to good works." (Heb. 10:24)

It would be less likely that these sort of people would force themselves into positions of power or authority if 'ordinary' Christians were awake and if they devoted themselves to the study of God's Word. Paul warned of the dangers of laziness and of letting other people take a lead or grasp for positions for which they are not called nor fitted. Writing to Timothy Paul warned. "For the time will come when they will not endure sound (wholesome) teaching, but after their own lusts shall heap to themselves teachers having itching ears. And they shall turn away their ears from the truth and shall be turned unto fables." (2Tim.4: 3,4)

The key to this is for more Christians to take up independent study, to challenge and to question the teachings of our pastors and teachers. The Bereans are mentioned in Acts chapter seventeen who though they listened attentively to the Apostle Paul did not accept the things he argued but checked up on him and what he said. As Luke has put it. "These were more noble than those in Thessalonica, in that they received the word with all readiness of mind, and searched the Scriptures daily whether those things were so." (Acts 17:10,11)

This is not a mere aside but is put in the Acts at this point to warn us to follow their example. Indeed we ought not to "have men's persons in admiration" for to do so seems to me to be bordering on idolatry. (Jude 16)

Our best safeguard is an attitude of mind which recognizes our own weaknesses. That is in particular to understand and admit that though we may believe the Bible to be right, our own particular opinions and interpretations may be flawed. We do well always to listen to others and to consider their opinions seriously even if we may disagree with them. Indeed we ought to listen more intently if they do disagree with us. They may, after all be right.

The Lord tells us clearly that the tares were not to be rooted up. This may seem at first a strange thing. Surely He would want all false teaching to be ruthlessly exposed and eradicated. The churches are not, however fascist states where law is administered with a heavy hand. It is the old problem exposed by the question, "but who shall guard the guardians?" Imagine how it is when groups in the churches take it upon themselves to define what is false and what is true. Imagine the hotly opposed partisans of this teacher and that. We already see this tendency at work in the apostolic age in Corinth and elsewhere. Paul wrote warning. "Now this I say, that every one of you says. 'I am of Paul, and I of

Apollos, and I of Cephas, and I of Christ'. Is Christ divided? Was Paul crucified for you? Or were you baptized in the name of Paul?" (1Cor.1: 12,13)

Paul does not take a hard line here, rather he appeals to their common sense and rationality. Even when they behave and speak irrationally we may use no other means against them. In an earlier verse he wrote. "Now I beseech you, brothers, by the Name of our Lord Jesus Christ, that you all speak the same thing and that there be no divisions among you, but that you be perfectly joined together in the same mind and in the same judgment." (v.10. See also Philipp. 1:27. 2:2)

There may be offences where the elders of a church, with the whole of the members, put a person out of fellowship; but this is a most serious undertaking and should not be done lightly. In general all matters ought to be dealt with in the open and by appeal only to Scripture. The exhortation to "be all of one mind" is something we are expected to be able to follow because we love the Lord Jesus and not as a legal requirement. We shall always have minor disagreements but they can, and ought, to be settled amicably by open discussion without quarrelling. Alas that is not how it works out in more cases than one could wish. We no doubt grieve the heart of God and become a scandal to the world which watches churches tear themselves apart. Because men love to have the pre-eminence or cannot admit they may be wrong.

The servants are warned that they must at times leave well alone lest worse happen. False teaching can only be dealt with by the use of salt, that is by the clear and rational application of truth. Elisha when his young men had gathered wild gourds from the field, faced a clear case of ignorance and a lack of discernment. (2Ki.4: 40) If we gather our doctrines from the world than we shall most certainly put our brothers and sisters in grave danger. I make the suggestion that the passion for sending our young people to Bible Colleges or to study theology at University is like gathering lapfuls of wild gourds in the field. After all "the field is the world". (Mt.13: 38)

It is only at the end of the age that, "the Son of Man shall send forth His angels". These shall do the reaping when the tares are to be burned. What a shock that will be for those who have acted as Lords over God's heritage and have enjoyed for years the adulation and admiration of others. (1Pe.5: 3.cf. 3Jn.9, 10) An eternity of "wailing and gnashing of teeth" is reserved for those who have behaved as such. The righteous, however, will find that one day everything will be put right and there will be rich rewards for those who have been faithful. (Mt.13: 40-43)

At the end of the age the angels do the reaping. This is one of those cases where we are given another glimpse of the ministry of angels. There are lots of cases like this and we do well to note them as we read. They then all add up to give us a larger and complete picture. In this case it is a picture of the work of the angels.

So full are the churches of a mixture of saved and unsaved people that to separate one from another would be impossible without hurting some or many of the children of the kingdom of God. The final sorting out has to wait for the end times. There has always been this unholy mixture in all ages but there is to be a sorting when Satan is to shut up in the abyss and the Beast and the False Prophet cast into the Lake of Fire.

We have to live with the situation in our age and carry on our witness as best we can. Remember faithful service will be rewarded. We must just do our best and leave what we cannot alter to the Lord to deal with. Or to send His angels as his ministers of justice to sort the chaff from the wheat. Here the Lord explains. "Let both grow together until the harvest and in the time of harvest

I will say to the reapers. 'Gather together first the tares and bind them in bundles to burn them but gather the wheat into my barn.'" (Mt.13: 30)

This event is described as the mysterious and sudden disappearance of certain people at that time of the end. This will probably happen after the cataclysmic events around Jerusalem where the Lord Himself, "treads the winepress of the wrath of God." This is how He explained it. "Then shall two be in the field the one shall be taken and the other left. Two woman shall be grinding at the mill the one shall be taken and the other left. Watch therefore for you know not what hour our Lord does come." (Mt.24: 40-42)

THE MUSTARD SEED

The opening of chapter thirteen of Mathew's Gospel is significant for the understanding of the seven parables of the Kingdom. "The same day went Jesus out of the house and sat by the sea. And great multitudes gathered unto him." (MT.13: 1, 2.KJV) From verse 46 of the previous chapter it is clear that he had been in a house with his disciples showing there a more intimate and private situation. This changed when the parables were about to be taught. The sea, in the Bible depicts the nations, always sinful, always at war, restless and discontented. These angry winds and waves can only be calmed by the Son of God as is demonstrated in chapter eight. (vv 23-27.) The winds, where the same word means 'spirit', also show us the influence of the demonic forces which do so much to shape this world's cultures. (for a more detailed study of this aspect of the subject the following verses may be helpful : Dan.7:2,3. Rev.13:1. Is 57:20. Prov.8:29. Mt.8:23-27. Mk4:37-41. Lk.8:23-25. Eph.2:2. 6:12. Psalm104: 4. John 5:19)

Also, in chapter 12 of Matthew we see a serious controversy with regard to the Sabbath. The upshot of this is the determination of the Pharisees to destroy the Lord Jesus. They also attribute the manifest power of God, seen in His miracles, to Satan so committing the unforgivable sin against the Holy Spirit. (Vv24, 31, 32)

With these points in mind we can begin our interpretation of the parables. Interpretation is helped by the fact that, though they were told to hide truth from unbelief, the Lord actually interpreted the Sower and the Tares for us. Even here there is a difference, the Sower being explained publicly to the crowds, but the Tares privately to the disciples back in the house. There is then, both a private aspect, for disciples only, and a public aspect to the interpretation and the application of the teaching of the parables.

This shows also the differing aspects of the two first parables. The first one is about the Sower in full public view working at sowing His seed in the open field. The second parable, that of the Tares and it is "while men slept". It deals with the secret, sly and underhand work of the evil one who sows confusion the false and the poisonous among the true.

There are seven of the parables telling us that here is a completeness and a finality. We have here a complete and accurate picture of God's dealing with the world and with His people. We are also shown how Satan attempts to subvert and to corrupt the work of the dissemination of the Word of God.

All seven parables are about the Kingdom of Heaven but in Mark and Luke four of them are about the Kingdom of God. For many these are the same but it may be worth wondering why the Holy Spirit chooses to use different terms if he did not mean different things. We have to make up our own minds about this point and the writer chooses not to be dogmatic. Daniel told Nebuchadnezzar that his mental illness (lycanthropy? See Hastings *Dictionary of Religion and Ethics*) was in order that he should learn, "that the heavens do rule". (Dan 4:26) The Watcher and the Holy One who caused this affliction was clearly of a number of such angelic beings appointed by God to punish human pride arrogance and hubris. (Again for a further and deeper investigation of this subject see the following: Job chapters 1 and 2. 1Ki 22:19-22 Dan 10:12,13,20. And Eph.6: 12)

A suggestion is that these two concepts overlap like two circles where parts of the circles are separate and parts share the same area. Entry into the Kingdom of God is by new birth. (John 3:3,5) Here is the sphere of God's direct rule. The heavenly powers, however, are those to whom God has delegated some of this responsibility and who rule on His behalf, some of these powers being fallen angels called, "the rulers of the darkness of this world, wicked spirits in the heavenlies". (Eph.6:12. KJ version ed. Newberry, margin)

The Sower shows us that the seed is, "the word of the Kingdom."(Verses19-23) John tells us that, "the whole world lies in the wicked one."(1Jn 5:19, see Newberry margin) In interpreting the Tares the Lord tells us that, "The field is the world," "The world is both under the control of Satan but it is the sphere of God's love, (Jn.3: 16) and of the Gospel. (Mt 28:19. Mk. 16:15) So there are two spiritual forces at work in the world and they are striving for the hearts, minds and souls of men.

The birds, in the case of the parables are clearly demonic forces whose aim is to subvert the preaching of the word and to corrupt those who hear it. In verse 19 it is "the Evil One who snatches away the seed that falls by the wayside. Luke gives a fuller rendering of the words of the Lord. "Then cometh the Devil and takes away the word out of their hearts lest they should believe and be saved."(Luke 8:12) Therefore in the parable under consideration we may safely assume that the birds are the same, evil spirits at work for their master Satan.

The immediate context is very helpful here in that; in Matthew chapter twelve we see the Pharisees not only rejecting the message of the Lord Jesus but actually plotting to destroy Him (v.14) this incident divides the Gospel into two halves for us. After chapter twelve the Lord is Israel's king in rejection. The parables are told because spiritual truth is hidden from the "wise and prudent," and, "revealed unto babes". Or, as the Lord Himself explained, to the disciples. "Because it is given unto you to know the mysteries of the kingdom of heaven, but to them it is not given."(Mt.13: 11) The most religious people in Israel had actually become the instruments of Satan and were soon to be joined by all the other religious leaders of all persuasions.

We, accustomed as we are to think of 'religion' as something generally good, often fail to understand how Satan has taken over the religious institutions of this world. This, of course is the obvious thing to do. We see in the Old Testament that the religions and the Ancient Middle East were the worship of the vile fertility gods and goddesses. These were worshipped with all sorts of sexual depravity. Not only was sacred prostitution of both males and females common, but that of children as well. To compound their abominations the religions of the ancient world also sacrificed their children to the cruel gods and goddesses which men had set up for themselves.

A second point is that, though Judaism was the only religion ever given by God, it had become the vehicle for human avarice and ambition. The very temple of God had, on the first occasion the Lord cleansed it, become, "a house of merchandise," and on the second, right at the end of His public ministry, "a den of thieves."(Jn.2: 13-17 Mt.21: 12,13) Here the temple, and the Jewish religion in general had become like the leprous house, condemned to be pulled down after two visits by the priest. (Lev.14:33-45) What had been planted by God through Moses, David and Solomon grew and became, like Babylon a "habitation of demons, and the hold of every foul spirit, and a cage of every unclean and hateful bird."(Rev.18:2)

Instead of being the guardians of Israel's law, its morals and its religious observances, the priests had become its exploiters. In also dancing attendance on the corrupt Herodian family and kow-towing to the ruling power of the Romans, they had become like noxious birds, with demons inciting them to take over religion and people for their master and to obstruct the coming of the Messiah.

Paul adds that it is one of the ploys of the evil one to disguise himself as an angel of light. Writing to the Corinthians he points out, concerning false teachers. "For such are false apostles, deceitful workers, transforming themselves into the apostles of Christ. And no marvel for Satan himself is transformed into an angel of light. Therefore it is no great thing if his ministers also be transformed as the ministers of righteousness." (2Cor. 11:13-15) It is hardly to be wondered at that we are misguided and misdirected by Bishops, Archbishops, Cardinals and Popes who claim to be the successors of the Apostles. In fact they are anything but. They in fact work for the enemy of all that is good and right.

In our own age the message of the Gospel of the Grace of God has similarly been subverted to a religion offering possible salvation with no certainty and that only by priestly intercession and by religious attendance and good works, thus making the work of Calvary of none effect. Even in apostolic days there were "false teachers," motivated and inspired by the demons, "even denying the Lord that bought them." (2Pet. 2:1)

Even from the first, Satan has worked in this way. So he appeared, in the beautiful and peaceful garden which God had planted, and brought about the downfall of the human race. The couple who should have been blissfully happy became, through his agency, the means of passing on suffering and death to their descendants. (Gen ch.3)

Later we see the human race and religion corrupted by the direct intervention of fallen angels who, "saw the daughters of men that they were fair and they took them wives of all which they chose." (Gen. 6:1,2) The promise of the Seed of the woman was not lost on Satan. Like hordes of vultures the demons were soon gathering to feast upon the corrupt and vulnerable human race. A travesty of the incarnation was brought into effect with beings neither angel nor human but a mixture of both as a result. The Bible refers to "giants" (v.4) but in Hebrew this is a word for "fallen ones". To their human dupes they were great heroes, Herakles (Hercules), Dionysus, and Apollo, who proclaimed oracles and were worshipped by deluded people in the ancient world as they are still worshipped today. Eve was, "the mother of all living," and she has become Satan's model for Isis, Aphrodite, or Venus, the goddess of motherhood, of licentiousness and of fertility. Today she is worshipped as Mary, the Mother of Jesus but she is in fact the ancient mother goddess. She has been bowed down to all over the world under a variety of names, also including Ishtar, Ashtoreth, Tannit, Kali, the Morrigan and Shing Mu. To her childless women pray and mothers in childbirth entreat her. To her men and women sacrifice their innocence and their purity.

This horrible fascination with idols is with us still and is increasing. Everywhere people wear amulets and charms, including crucifixes and other, so-called, "Christian" symbols. Simply put, Satan likes to take over whatever is originally of God. Even when the Lord, to demonstrate His compassion and His power performed miracles of healing he had to silence the voices of demons who, "came out of many, crying out, and saying, 'Thou art the Christ the Son of God.' And He, rebuking them, suffered them not to speak; for they knew He was Christ." (Lk. 4:40,41) Satan is all too eager to patronise what is of God in order to subvert it for his own ends and to misdirect the worship rightly due only to God to himself.

Our only defence against such determined Satanic attack is in reliance upon prayer and the study and practice of the Bible. We have so much to do. Of ourselves we have no power and no wisdom but we depend totally upon the Lord and we believe in His Word. May we thank God, "Who gives us the victory through our Lord Jesus Christ." (1Cor. 15:57)

In our world today there have always been sacred wells and springs. The old gods and goddesses, who came into human culture

70

after the flood, still lurk in the woodlands and the mountain and in the temples where pagan rites are celebrated. They are being recalled by neo pagan movements and by the renewed interest in all religions except Biblical Christianity. Our fellow humans are taking up with enthusiasm this revival of interest in religion and the demons see to it that it all serves to keep people from the love of the Lord Jesus Christ. Even a leader of a major denomination of Christendom has been enrolled as a druid, the order of priests of the ancient Celtic religion.

The demons, driven out by the evangelical movement in the eighteenth and nineteenth centuries are now, not just trickling back, but are flooding our world and bringing back with them seven others worse than themselves.(See Mt. 12:43-45) If that was true of the time the Lord spoke and it is true of our own age, then it is true in all ages. Darwinism led the way in suggesting that Biblical belief was not "scientific". As a result people do not believe in nothing, rather they believe in anything. Instead of doing things because they are right they do them because they 'feel good'.

With the "salt of the earth" (Mt.5: 13) already corrupt it is no wonder that Paul's terrible vision of the last days is coming true. "Perilous times," when, "men shall be lovers of their own selves, covetous, boasters, proud, blasphemous, disobedient to parents, unthankful, unholy, without natural affection, trucebreakers, false accusers, incontinent, fierce, despisers of those that are good, traitors, heady, puffed up, lovers of pleasure more than lovers of God,…" (2Tim. 3:1-5)

The world is full of religions but they have their origins in the cunning and twisted mind of the Evil One, a liar and a murderer from the beginning.(Jn.8:43-46) We do well to heed the Holy Spirit's warning through the Apostle Paul that, "in the latter times some shall depart from the faith, giving heed to seducing spirits and doctrines of demons."

Any work of God tends, by the world, to be seen as weak and feeble. So it is that the mustard seed represents something God does in the world. The mustard seed is very small. The plant referred to was the *sinapis nigra* and, in a good soil it can grow to a height of ten or twelve feet. Birds do indeed "lodge in its braches" and, with its minute seed exactly fulfils the purpose of the parable.

The work of the Lord Jesus is despised in our day, just as the words of the prophets and their warnings were ignored. Nevertheless the seed grows to an enormous size for what it is but when it is full grown it attracts the demonic forces which take over what God started.

We can see how the small beginning has gradually grown into the cancerous growth that is Christendom, with its sects and systems, with its high priests in their fish-head hats and rich regalia. With its millions of confused, dazzled and bewildered followers, believing the words of priests who neither know the power of God nor believe the Scriptures.

The church has settled down in the world, becoming an idolatrous institution worshipping the empty gods and goddesses of the ancient world with the same violence and immorality; based upon the same lies and the same ridiculous ceremonies and posturing. The demonic birds very soon took up residence in its branches as they saw the possibilities for perversion of the truth. We are now down a long way, indeed nearly at the end of the road leading to Babylon and the world ruler soon to be foisted on the whole of earth's population, by his master, Satan.

THE PARABLE OF THE LEAVEN

"Another parable spake He unto them. The Kingdom of the heavens is like unto leaven which a woman took and hid in three measures of meal, till the whole was leavened." (Mt.13:33)

People who ought to know better see this parable as showing the working of the Gospel in the world and they understand, against all the obvious and rational evidence, that the Gospel will in the end prevail and the whole world will, at last be converted. Pigs might fly and crayfish might as well learn to whistle. This is not about the Gospel, but like the other parables which precede it is about the cosmic conflict which is working itself out in the churches, and the missions which take on the might of Satan.

We have had two thousand years since this parable was told and there is less sign of the world being converted now than there was at the beginning. Every age in which God has dealt with men in His grace and in various ways has started off with a great demonstration of God's power and has ended in dismal failure and widespread corruption.

The conversion of the world must wait until the Lord Jesus returns. When He does then, "every knee shall bow and every tongue confess that Jesus Christ is Lord, to the glory of God the Father." Until that time we wrestle with the mighty powers of darkness and count our small victories and our defeats. (Philipp. 2:9-11)

In the meanwhile the few here and there are saved. We on our part, in order to understand how God is really working must investigate the meaning of the word 'leaven' (yeast) and who and how it is that it is introduced into the wholesome teaching, symbolized by the three measures of meal. Then we need to consider what its effects are.

The best way to get to the true meaning of a word or a phrase is to see how it is used in the Bible. Unless you have a stupendous memory for what you read there is no chance of that. Even with such a memory we cannot get behind the vagaries of the translators unless we can find a way to follow and original word or phrase through its every occurrence.

To begin with, we find that leaven was banned from the Passover and for the following week of the Feast of Unleavened bread. Its literal meaning is 'something fermented'. The fermentation spreads, feeding on its host. Soon the host food becomes rotten and smells of corruption. It is unfit for human consumption. Leaven was also forbidden in any of the sacrifices; no sacrifice was to be burned with leaven. (Lev. 6:17)

The one exception to this rule was with regard to the two wave loaves offered during the Feat of Pentecost, or Weeks, 'a new gift offering'. There is a good reason for this which is to do with the harvest but to pursue that path is to lead us away from the discussion of the parable. (See Ex. 12:15. 13:3,7. 34:25. Lev. 2:11. 23:17. Deut. 16:3. And cf. Amos 4:5)

There are actually two words translated leaven. 'Seor' is also used in this way. (Ex.12:15. Deut. 16:14) In the New Testament we get this clear picture confirmed. "A little leaven leavens the whole lump." (1Cor. 5:6-8. Gal. 5:9) In both these passages the word is used to describe an evil and corrupting process. In both Matthew's Gospel and in Luke's we find the Lord comparing the teaching of the Pharisees with leaven. "Then understood they how that He bade them beware not of the leaven of bread but of the doctrine (teaching) of the Pharisees and of the Sadducees." (Mt.16:6-12) Luke says how the Lord explicitly stated. "Beware ye of the leaven of the Pharisees which is hypocrisy." (Lk. 12:1)

These things, symbolized by the yeast, corrupt the things and the people of God but they are also at work in the world generally and so they also corrupt everything human; there is nothing and no one that is immune. Western society is a case in point, or more particularly British society. Successive revivals of Christian thinking, since the Civil War, brought about a society which lived with the Bible as its basic building block. We had a clear set of absolutes. Even people who were not Christians, and there were many of them, at least believed the moral values taught in the Bible. For that reason it was possible to carry on a discussion with everyone. You could for instance point out that slavery was wrong and that God condemned it. You might, in this context, refer to Exodus 21:16 which showed that God condemned to death anyone who kidnapped another human being and sold them as property. This is why Britain was so successful in ending the abominable trade in human beings; then, finally the institution of slavery itself.

Indeed one of the most successful of the many Reform Movements was that to stop the slave trade and was eventually to stop slavery itself in the British Empire Other nations, then reluctantly followed suit though they did not want to. For more than one hundred and fifty years the movement's supporters argued, raised awareness and campaigned until at last enough people were convinced, even some of the merchants who had grown rich on the trade eventually admitted they had been wrong.

In 1807 the trade in slaves was stopped and in 1833 slavery itself was ended. After a while Spain, France and Portugal followed suit but the USA needed a civil war to resolve matters. The Islamic nations lingered on as the last to reject the gross injustice and searing cruelty being inflicted upon millions of human beings. Even then the attempt was halfhearted and insincere.

There was no violence to this peaceful and gentle revolution; though revolution it was. It was a complete change of heart, mind and practice. Christian people faithfully and patiently kept up their protests and their arguments and finally prevailed. Some will argue that the movement did not go far enough. This is true, but it does not hide the fact that Christian persuasion triumphed whereas the political revolutions of the past and the present have never succeeded in doing what they set out to do. Rather they have always made matters worse. Lenin and Stalin brought about a greater tyranny than ever there was under the Czars in Russia. Napoleon claimed to personify the will of the people and plunged the whole of Europe into bloodshed, terror and war.

By their witness Christian people act as salt in society and bring about more good than ever do the legislators. "You are the salt of the earth," said the Lord Jesus; then He warned, "but if the salt has lost its savour (lit, to become foolish) wherewith shall it be salted? It is thenceforth good for nothing but to be cast out and to be trodden under foot of men." (Mt. 5:13. See also Lk.14:34)

So much for Christian witness in Britain today. The salt has gone off; it is no longer pungent and effective. We have compromised and false teachings such as evolution, and other corrupting forces are in the ascendancy. Pornography is everywhere, certainly in the popular press, while the family is despised, society broken, fraud, lies and hypocrisy commonplace and more blatant day by day.

The leaven has long been at work and as in a previous parable; the demonic birds are making their homes in the branches of what ought to have been devoted to God. All of us who have eyes to see are fully aware of this depraved state of affairs. Few try to do something about it. Most are sitting helpless weeping into their handkerchiefs while a good number avert their eyes and pretend it is not happening.

So we agree that the leaven has been at work, is working and ought to be stopped. Let us next try to decide who and what the woman is who so adroitly introduced it into the "three measures of meal". She may be understood in a variety of ways none of which may be popular with political correctness.

So who was it who first listened to the honeyed tones of the old serpent in the garden? "Yea! Has God said?...You shall not surely die." Well He did, and we do; die I mean. Eve listened to the Deceiver and not to God. Eve was first in the transgression. She was deceived, Adam was not. (1Tim. 2:14,15) We shall find three other notable cases of women who hid the leaven and who brought about immense suffering as a result.

However Eve was the first. What she did affected, or perhaps infected, three measures of meal. There are broadly speaking three main eras. First the world up to the flood. Then the world of the patriarchs and the giving of the Law. Finally the world of grace when the Lord Jesus visited it and so a door is open in heaven. (Rev.4:1) "The world that then was," perished in the flood for, "it was corrupt before God, and was filled with violence". (Gen. 6:11) After that the world of Abraham and his descendants received God's Law. A Law not they, nor us, could keep, a law which condemned us all as sinners. "For by the Law is the knowledge of sin." (Rom 3:19,20)

At last came the Lord Jesus to "put away sin by the sacrifice of Himself". The benefits of His work and of His blessings are with us now and will continue until God creates a "New Heavens and a New Earth wherein dwells righteousness" (2Pe. 3:13. Rev. 21:1,5)

Eve started all the trouble but neither was Adam without blame. In pagan mythology we have the story of Pandora who, filled with burning curiosity, opened the box entrusted to her husband and set free into the world all the evils imaginable all of which could not be called back nor locked up again.

Eve has had a few notable followers, among which are Jezebel, the wife of King Ahab, Athaliah her daughter and the Jezebel who taught wickedness in the church at Thyatira. (Rev 2:18ff) There is a certain overlap in the parables of the tares and of the leaven. Both Jezebel and Ahab were undoubtedly "children of the Evil One," thus fulfilling the parable of the tares. On the other hand, in that they were both guilty of spreading ungodly and corrupt practices among the people they ruled they were also introducing leaven.

Here is what the Biblical history says about Ahab and Jezebel. "Ahab the son of Omri did evil in the sight of the lord above all that were before him. And it came to pass, as if it had been a light thing for him to walk in the sins of Jeroboam the son of Nebat that he took to wife Jezebel, the daughter of Ethbaal King of the Sidonians." (1Ki.16:30,31) This passage goes on to say how Ahab worshipped and served Baal, built altars and a temple for Baal and then built a grove where the fertility goddess was worshipped. By introducing the worship of Baal and Ashtoreth into Israel he caused corruption to spread. This was the corruption of the vile fertility worship where even children were sacrificed to the idols.

Athaliah the daughter of Ahab and Jezebel was married to the son of Jehoshaphat, the good King whose mistake was to make an alliance with the evil Ahab King of Israel in Samaria. Since alliances were often sealed by a marriage this gave the forces of darkness the chance to have a foothold in Judah. It was not just that the corrupt and depraved Athaliah introduced Baal worship to Jerusalem but that she also murdered all the seed royal so the succession to the throne of Judah would be hers. The disastrous alliance with the northern kingdom caused the death of the son of Athaliah thus giving her the opportunity which she had obviously been long contemplating. "And when Athaliah the mother of Ahaziah saw that her son was dead, she arose and destroyed all the seed royal. (2Ki.11:1)

Her plans however were thwarted in what can only be the overruling work of God. The High priest's wife, herself of the royal family, and her husband kept the youngest son of the late King hidden in the temple. When he was old enough he was proclaimed king with the High Priest and others as regents. Athaliah, naturally was executed much as her mother had been when Jehu led his rebellion.

Much later, at the end of the first century a.d., a prophetess arose in the church at Thyatira. She, like her namesake, introduced evil and false teaching among the people of God. The Lord Jesus spoke of her saying that she had been allowed, "to teach and seduce My servants to commit fornication and to eat things sacrificed to idols". (Rev.2:20) For a woman to take this position was quite wrong of course, but she did not even teach any good things. Nor for that matter do we hear that the people acted like the Bereans and, "searched the Scriptures daily whether those things were so." (Acts 17:10, 11) Had they done so they would surely have found that the teaching was wrong. As today they were sermon tasters who never questioned what the speaker said.

All this is confirmed to us by a vision of the last days and the coming of the Great tribulation. We may even now be seeing the scene being set for its fulfillment. Zechariah, in chapter five of his prophecy recounts his vision of the Ephah which is carried by two unclean birds, " To build it an house in the land of Shinar (Babylon) and it shall be established." The Ephah is the symbol of commerce and we already see the capitalist system reaching out its tentacles all over the world to bring every nation within its grasp. Sitting in the middle of the Ephah is a woman sealed in by a talent of lead. The talent is also a symbol of commerce but this is of lead and not of silver or of gold. It is, ultimately worthless. The woman, like Eve is the bringer of disaster to the world. (Zechariah 5:5-11)

The rapacity of the rich and powerful is getting worse. At the same time the minds of the population are being destroyed and the rot is setting in while our children are still young for capitalism owns the entertainment industry and the drugs and alcohol industries as well. The world has seen pleasure as the ultimate good; for human philosophy has nothing to offer and has no answers to the big questions. Together with all this comes, also owned by capitalism, is the trade in pornography and, seeing human sexuality simply as pleasure, humans consequently have learned that it is good and right to indulge themselves in this.

Fornication, as described in the Bible. may have been real and sexual or symbolic of idolatry. In either case it was and is wrong. But does spiritual fornication end there? How many young people are out pubbing and clubbing on a Saturday night and in the morning, pretending to worship God. They enjoy the same wild and carnal music they were dancing to the night before? How many of our young people are engaged in active sexual activity with no rebuke from the leaders of the church? And in so doing are they not destroying their own capacity for the enjoyment of God given marital intimacy?

The churches are full of self-styled and publicly accredited teachers and prophets who tell the people that church should be 'fun' and that they are to be happy. So by implication anything which gives them a fleeting sense of euphoria is deemed to be acceptable and approve of by God since they feel 'happy' when doing it. Anyone can get a very effective sense of happiness after several glasses of whisky or a selection of the mind altering pills on offer at the clubs they frequent. We ought to consider seriously that the Lord Jesus was, "a Man of sorrows and acquainted with grief." And that the "fruit of the Spirit is (among other things) Self control."

Finally in chapter seventeen of Revelation we find a horrifying vision. It is of a woman who holds a cup in her hand with which she makes the nations drunk. "And the woman was arrayed in purple and scarlet colour, and decked with gold and precious stones and pearls, having a golden cup in her hand full of abominations and filthiness of her fornication." (Rev 17:4-6)

Commentators differ as to who and what this woman is. Some argue she is the church of Rome. They may have a point but it is only part of the truth. Certainly that evil system is guilty of being "drunk with the blood of the saints and with the blood of the martyrs of Jesus". (v.6) The middle ages were witness to the martyrdom of many who loved the Lord Jesus and rejected the worship of the 'mother goddess' and the corruptions of the religious system of Rome. However verse 5 tells us that she is. "Mystery Babylon the great, the mother of harlots and abominations of the earth." She is also the woman in the ephah and controlling it from her throne in Babylon.

We see her origin in the tower built in the first years after the flood. Where Satan tried to impose, with the aid of the evil, power-hungry Semiramis, a universal nationhood and a universal religion. (Gen.11:1-4) Allied to this was to be a world government and with that a world-wide control over all people.

This 'spirit of Anti-Christ has been at work for many millennia now and is working up to its final point. It would be nice if we could, unaided throw it off but as with the original Babel and with all the Babels which have been built since, we are too blind or too lazy even to try. The woman is riding upon a seven headed wild beast which has ten crowns. It is the final stage of the final World

81

Empire, the empire of Rome. It is Rome at its final and ignoble end. Yes! Soon the trumpet will sound and we shall be taken up. The trumpet will then also signal the final years of judgment and the whole world will support the wild beast. Through this time of trouble such as never was experienced by this sad world before, Israel shall be brought to repentance.

At the beginning of this final prophetic week Anti-Christ, will come to power and first will seem to be a beneficial ruler so that he restores peace and extends his power by peaceful means. Then in the middle of the week, that is after forty-two months he will show himself to be the monster he really is. He will break the treaty with Israel and overthrow everything religious. He will sit himself in the Holy of Holies in the Jewish temple in Jerusalem, to demonstrate that he is God. Paul writing to the Thessalonians remarks on this. He wrote. "Let no man deceive you by any means. For that day shall not come, except there come a falling away first, and that Man of Sin be revealed, the son of perdition. Who opposes and exalts himself above all that is called God or that is worshipped. So that he as God sits in the temple of god showing himself that he is God." (2Thess. 2:3,4)

During the first phase the woman supports the Beast but as soon as this happens he gives authority to his subject and client Kings to attack the world-wide religion which the woman has become. "And the ten horns which thou sawest upon the wild Beast, these shall hate the whore, and shall make her desolate and naked, and shall eat her flesh and burn her with fire." (Rev.17:16,17)

From being in control of the secular powers, she has everything stripped away from her and the Beast himself becomes the sole object of worship; so that, "all the world wondered after the Beast. And they worshipped the Dragon which gave power unto the Wild Beast and they worshipped the Wild Beast, saying, 'who is like unto the Wild Beast, who is able to make war with him?'" (Rev 13:3,4)

Interestingly enough we see the world's religions slowly but surely coming together. We see the sects and systems of Christendom coming together and putting themselves under the malign influence of Rome and eventually, no doubt, under its supreme power. It may not be long before we see a great religious combination coming into being which will exert a corrupt and Satanic control over the minds and the hearts of all people.

The leaven is working and the whole world is becoming corrupt, though the world does not see it as that. As the corruption spreads the perverted thinking of world leaders and their followers gets increasingly bent to the will of Satan and to that of his demons. It is not his will however to raise the Vatican to supreme world power though that is what the Vatican has long coveted.

Satan blinds the minds of those who do not believe. (2Cor.4; 3,4) Chapter thirteen of Revelation shows us how The Wild Beast's Minister of Propaganda and of Public Enlightenment uses his powers. He causes the Dragon and the Wild Beast to become the objects of universal worship by doing wonders and miracles. "He does great wonders so that he makes fire come down from heaven on the earth in the sight of men, and deceives them that dwell on the earth by means of those miracles which he has power to do in the sight of the Wile Beast. Saying to them that dwell on the earth that they should make an image to the Wild Beast which had the wound by a sword and did live and he had power to give life to the image of the Wild Beast that the image of the Wild Beast should both speak and cause that as many as would not worship the image of the Wild Beast should be killed." (Re 13:11-15)

The event, which starts the destruction of all religions also signals the assertion by the Beast that he is God and there are no other gods or goddesses so he alone is to be worshipped, is an assassination attempt on the Beast which he survives in spite of its apparent success. (See Rev.13:3. 2Thess 2:9. Zech.11:17)

This means that he claims to have been killed and then resurrected. He takes over the Jewish temple and shows himself to be God by sitting on a throne in the Holy Place and receiving the worship of everyone, including the apostates of Israel. These already three and a half years earlier will have "made a covenant with death and an agreement with Hades." They think that this treaty will have made them safe but they fail to realise that the Beast is utterly ruthless and treaty breaking is a matter of little importance to him.(See Isaiah 28:14,15, 18,19. Dan.9:27) Like all the dictators and tyrants of every time, his only aim is What is expedient to raise himself to the thorn of the world and his master the devil to the height of the heavens.

Here is the working of the leaven. It has been working for a long time and it has been working in different ways in order to bring Satan's plans to fruition. It has brought about a delusion which is to be world-wide. It is a delusion which at last brings the world to believe the ultimate lie that Satan is God and that the Beast, the Anti-Christ, is the true Christ and the world's rightful ruler. Satan purposed "to be like the Most High". He tried to take over in Heaven but failed and was cast out. Now he is working to be god on earth, as with a seething rage, he goes about to "blind the minds of those who believe not". (2Cor.4:3.) So it is his aim that the world acknowledges him as god and worships him as god. (Isaiah 14:12-14.)

In a statement, one which we can easily miss, mistaking it simply as the throw away remark; the Lord Jesus showed how He was fully aware of this process going on when He was on earth. Here it is as John recorded the very words. "I am come in My Father's

84

Name and you receive me not. If another shall come in his own name, him you will receive." (Jn.5:43)

The leaven is working now and it seems as if nothing can oppose it nor halt the process of corruption. However salt is the remedy for salt kills off the agents of corruption and preserves those foods which so easily go bad and inedible. "You are the salt of the earth," the Lord Jesus cautioned then went on, "but if the salt have lost his savour wherewith shall it be salted? It is thenceforth good for nothing but to be cast out and to be trodden under foot by men." (Mt.5:13)

He also goes on to say that we are also the 'Light of the World'. What a great level of responsibility God has given us. How badly we often let Him down. Is it that the salt is no longer effective that the rot sets in at a rapidly quickening pace? We surely must look to ourselves must we not? Is it that our Christian witness in the west has become weak and effete? How many of my readers (if any) and how many more who would never dream of picking up a book to read, spend many hours every evening watching television and rubbish on television at that. Most of their leisure time I suspect Christians sit in a semi-trance before the idiots looking box? How many of the pursuits we follow are trivial and pointless? How much of our time is taken away from our serious role in the world so that the most important thing is neglected? Our time is given over to the god of immediate gratification and of conspicuous consumption.

We may also, I think see all this from another similar and related aspect. The leaven is hid in three measures of meal. In Numbers 15:9 and through chapters 28 and 29 we see that three tenth deals of fine flour is the measure of the gift offering for the larger sacrifices. One may argue that the fine flour tells about the Lord Jesus. The various sacrifices required are to do, in their size and quantity with the amount of responsibility of the one offering the sacrifice. Thus for a priest or a prince a larger animal is required for sacrifice. Three is the number of revelation, of the Trinity and of resurrection. The person and work of the Lord Jesus are the prime targets for the malevolence of Satan and he attacks these doctrines with all his vast intellect and brings men into bondage to cults and to teachings which undermine the truth. Oppositions of Science (knowledge-gnosis), the Bible says, "falsely so called". (1Tim.6: 20) It is Satan's purpose to ridicule the Lord Jesus and to reduce Him to the state of a nonentity. He will thus be able to introduce his Christ to a gullible and deluded world.

Anything which corrupts, confuses and destroys the doctrines of the Trinity and of the Deity of the Lord Jesus and of His saving work on the cross, is the leaven introduced into the find flour by the woman, the goddess, the evil and false religious system which at the last will itself be overthrown and destroyed by its creator so he alone can have all the glory.

A BREAK AND A CHANGE

The first four parables are told to the crowds by the side of the Sea of Galilee. "Then Jesus sent the multitude away and went into the house. And his disciples came unto him saying, "Declare unto us the parable of the tares in the field". The Lord then gave the interpretation which we have considered and finished his explanation with the words. "Who has ears to hear, let him hear." (Mt.13:43) The Lord tells us His interpretation but it is our responsibility to take it all in. There are plenty who listen to sermons but few of them learn much. There are plenty who make an effort to read the Bible but their reading is desultory and lacks serous thought and questioning. Again the Bereans of Acts 17 are our examples of serious, committed learners. These last are the ones who have "ears to hear".

There remains three more to be told and they are told to the disciples in private, in the house, cut off from the multitude. Seven is the perfect number but it is divided into four and three. Four is the universal number and shows us the cosmic conflict going on in various ways. The Sower and the Tares are clearly related and the Mustard Seed and the Leaven are similar to each other, so the universal number, the number of the world is seen to be a place of witness and testimony.

The final three are different. These three parables show us the work of the Lord Jesus. Again we may see the number divided into two and one. One is the number of unity and supremacy so these last three parables tell us how the lord finally brings things in this world and ultimately in the universe under His control, that He may be supreme. On day, "every knee shall bow and every tongue confess that Jesus Christ is Lord to the glory of God the Father." (Is.45:23. Rom.14:11. Philipp.2:10) Writing to the Corinthians

Paul explains how the lord Jesus "delivers up the kingdom to the Father that God may be all in all." (1Cor.15:24-28)

Here then is the purpose of the final three parables in that they complete what was begun in the first part of the series of events with the four parables. They tell us how the Lord sees the work of salvation and how He achieves his victory winning in it a rich and valuable booty from the defeat of Satan.

Three is also the number of the Trinity and of abundant witness and testimony so those matters are briefly but fully covered by these parables.

THE TREASURE HID IN A FIELD

"Again the Kingdom of Heaven is like unto treasure hid in a field, the which, when a man has found , he hides and for joy thereof goes and sells all he has and buys that field." (Mt.13:44)

When explaining the parable of the tares the Lord stated. "The field is the world." This, from the immediate context, tells us how we are to interpret the parable. The treasure is hid 'in the world'. Some people think that the reference to the world means the Hebrew word 'arets'. They conclude that this means Israel, this is not so. The word translated world here is Kosmos, so if the "field is the world," then it has to be more than the land of Israel and more than this planet. Clearly the world Kosmos may be taken to mean the universe since with these last three parables we are looking at things from a heavenly point of view. That is we are seeing from God's point of view, from outside the universe and what we have is a picture of things which is universal.

The man who sees the treasure and sells all that He has so He can buy the field is the Lord Jesus. Amidst all the multitudes rushing about, carried to and fro by every wind of teaching, pushed here and there by the crowds and by their opinions and constrained by social and political pressures, the Lord sees those who constitute His special treasure. To gain this treasure he gave up everything and, paid the only price which would buy that treasure. The treasure is so precious, so valuable it is priceless. But only the Lord sees that, all else look with scorn on what God loves, what God values.

Here however is what the Lord Jesus paid. Paul explains. He, "made Himself of no reputation and took upon him the form of a servant (slave) and was made in the likeness of men. And being found in fashion as a man He humbled Himself and became obedient unto death even the death of the cross." (Philippians 3;5-8) This is how Peter tells explains it. "Forasmuch as you know that you were not redeemed with corruptible things as silver and gold, from your vain behavior received by tradition from your fathers. But with the precious Blood of Christ as of a lamb without blemish and without spot." (1Peter 1:18,19)

Before we look deeper into this we also have to consider what many may say, that how is it that the Lord had to buy the field at the cost of His precious Blood? How is it that He could not just take it? If the field which is the world is already owned by the Lord Jesus since He is its Creator why go through all this. The fact is that a usurper is still in control. The Evil One asserts his authority over the field which is the Universe. He does so because he wrested its control from God's regent long ago in the Garden of Eden. God's Regent was Adam and the Lord has bought him back as well as all of his descendants who wish to be saved. Even if none were saved, because of what the Lord has done God is now able to dismiss Satan into the Lake of Fire and to create a New Heavens and a New Earth.

We have the statement written by John that, "the whole world lies in the Wicked One". (1Jn.5:19) This is a simple statement of fact. Satan controls this world as if he owned it. We should note in passing that the A.V. translates this as "the whole world lies in wickedness but the correct rendering is, as I have given above, "the Wicked One".

From the fall Satan controlled this world. When the Lord met him in the wilderness he offered the Lord a simple and painless solution to the matter of control over the world. He must have thought, in his pride and his arrogance, that he could buy off the Lord Jesus by giving Him a way round the sufferings and the horror of a death on the cross, being utterly alone and bearing the sin of the whole world. Here is the bargain he offered the Lord Jesus. It also seems likely that he was so full of himself that he actually believed that he had a possibility of success. Ezekiel records God's comment on the subject. After describing the power, intellect, and beauty of Satan he says. "Thine heart was lifted up because of thy beauty, thou hast corrupted they wisdom by reason of thy brightness." (2:17)

"And the Devil, taking Him up into an high mountain showed Him all the kingdoms of the world in a moment of time. And the devil said to Him. 'All this authority will I give Thee and the glory of them, for that is delivered unto me, and to whomsoever I will, I give it. If Thou, therefore, wilt worship me, all shall be Thine.'" (Mt.4:8-10. Lk.4:5-8)

The Lord Jesus did not answer this challenge with a straight denial. Remembering that he was and is The Truth, we have to recognise the significance of this. That he did not deny the validity of Satan's claim to own "all the kingdoms of the world," shows that it was not a false one. The Lord's silence on that matter confirms what John had written though by then the Lord had actually defeated Satan though His victory was not then put into effect for lots of very good reasons.

Because, at the very beginning Satan had brought about the fall of Adam and Eve he took away from them the right to rule the earth as God had given them. Satan, Adam's conqueror, then took over the rule and asserted it in his blasphemous offer to the Lord Jesus. Eventually the Lord will take what is now His. .Passages in Revelation, concerning the end of this era, show us this. John wrote in Revelation as follows. "And the seventh angel sounded and there came great voices in Heaven saying. 'The kingdoms of this world are become the kingdoms of our Lord and of His Christ; and He shall reign forever and forever.'" (Rev.11:15)

We should also note that it is for us to engage also in the heavenly conflict and to win. Adam may have been defeated but his descendants now fight alongside the heavenly angels as soldiers commanded by the Lord Jesus. (1Tim.1:18, 19. 2Tim.2:3,4)

The following chapter develops this theme, telling of the great future battle in the Heavenlies between the powers of Satan and those of Michael, the great angel prince, who stands for the nation of Israel. (Rev.12:7-9. Cf.Dan.12: 1,2) Michael is both Israel's guardian angel and the nation's representative. This event signals the beginning of the end for this world as we know it, for Satan's rule and the count-down starts for both the kingdom of the Anti Christ and for the salvation of Israel. By this time, of course, the church which is His body will have been taken up into heaven to be with Him.

It is a testing time for Israel when the godly remnant is protected and the rest go through the fires until they finally "mourn for Him Whom they pierced". (Zech.12:10) Finally when, with "all nations gathered to destroy Jerusalem," the Lord Jesus Himself, "shall go forth and fight against those nations as when He fought in the day of battle." (14:3) That is when Satan will be bound and consigned to the abyss until, after the end of the thousand years when he is to be, "cast into the Lake of Fire". (Rev.20: 1-3,10)

At the present time we see the Lord Jesus as the man who "sold all He had and bought the field". It would have been in his power to destroy the world and all the sinners with it. However He did not. There was treasure hid in the field. It was both the church and the Nation of Israel. Both these are precious to Him.

He sold all that He had in order to buy the field. He, "made Himself of no reputation and took the form of a slave." What wonderful grace. To lay aside all that was His, to become a man and then to submit to the excruciating death of the cross. And more; to have laid upon Him the iniquity of us all. All that He had as God the Son was laid aside that He might become a man and die to save the world. In doing so all those who "came to God by Him" were saved and are His Treasure. By the same token Israel too one day soon is going to be saved when they finally "mourn for Him Whom they pierced". (Phil2:7,8. Is.53:6.Zech.12:10)

Here is how Isaiah has explained it prophetically. "He is despised and rejected of men. A man of sorrows and acquainted with grief." The prophecy then continues after a few lines. "Surely He has borne our griefs and carried our sorrows. Yet we did esteem Him stricken, smitten of God and afflicted. But He was wounded for our transgressions; He was bruised for our iniquities. The chastisement of our peace was upon Him and with His stripes we are healed." (Is.53:3-5)

The vast, indeed infinite, price the Lord Jesus paid to set the world free and to obtain that treasure which, all unknown to the world was hidden there, is explained by Peter in the passage from his first letter quoted above. Silver and gold are the world's currency. They are metals which in worldly, earthly terms do not rust. However the price the Lord paid, that of His Precious blood, is infinitely more valuable than any sum of money which men could imagine.

This parable, like the one which follows it, the parable of the Pearl of Great Price, gives another aspect of the work of the Lord Jesus and of the view of the situation of the Kingdom of the Heavens where God and Satan are in conflict. The Parable of the Tares shows us how Satan undermines what God has set up and how thereby he confuses issues so men fail to see clearly what God is doing. Satan blinds the minds of those who believe not. (2Cor.4:3,4) The tares are the false among the true. People think they are real Christians but they are not. They are similar to the true, they look like the true, but they are not the true; they are full of poison and, unlike the wheat are unwholesome, unfit for anything.

A different aspect is seen in the Parable where we find the pearl of great price for sale and bought by the merchant who sells everything else He possesses in order to buy the pearl

The Lord speaks in parables to the people, and then interprets his words to the disciples, because to them, to the men of the world, it is not given to understand. Only those, the "eyes of whose understanding have been enlightened," may discern these things. (Ephesians1:18) They do not see the treasure when they see the Lord's people; they are merely just other workers, neighbours or men and women in the street, no different to anyone else. If they do see us as different it is folk with rather strange ideas like believing in God or in Creation and not in evolution. They see us as naïve or eccentric, or both and not as treasure, not as part of something of great price.

When Malachi had finished warning Israel of their wrongdoings and had accused them of robbing God he was inspired to suddenly change tack as it were and to come out with a complete change of mood. It is suddenly complementary and so lovely that you feel you want to sing. Here is what God had to say in the midst of all the warnings and recriminations. It is at the end of chapter three. "Then they that feared the Lord spake often one to another. And The Lord hearkened and heard it and a book of remembrance was written before Him, for them that feared the Lord and that thought upon His Name. And they shall be Mine saith the Lord of Hosts, in that day when I make up my Jewels (special treasure)." (vv16,17)

Here is God's special treasure. This too is the Pearl of Great Price which is our next parable. Imagine a group of persecuted Christians, say in North Korea or one of the many other countries where it is considered wrong to be a Christian. The Lord does not look down upon those people and in so doing relishes their devotion and their love. He does not enter silently from heaven into their discussion of the wonderful things of God. No! He does not. He is there with them and among them. He told His disciples "Where two or three are gathered together unto My Name, there am I in the midst of them." (Mt.18:20)

Here is a principle which is hardly at all understood. It is not even understood by the true Christians who ought to know better. It is a principle which goes through the Bible from the Torah to the Revelation. It is the principle of the Place of the Name. Warning the children of Israel against the idolatry of the nations and of their separation from all superstition and corruption, Moses wrote. "Ye shall not do so (worship like the nations worship their idols) unto the Lord your God. But unto the place which the Lord your God shall choose out of all your tribes to put His name there, even unto His habitation shall you seek and thither thou shalt come. And thither you shall bring your burnt offerings and your sacrifices and your tithes and heave offerings of your hand and your vows and your freewill offerings and the firstling of your herds and of your flocks. And there you shall eat before the Lord your God and you shall rejoice in all that you put your hand unto. You and your households wherein the lord thy God has blessed thee." (Deut.12: 4-7)

When they spent forty years in the wilderness they had a tent, the tabernacle. Later Solomon built the temple and then, when the age of grace commenced, then God's house was among His people. Not a building made with hands as Solomon had said when he dedicated the temple he had built. (1Ki.8: 15,16,27-29. Acts 7:48. 17:24) Now God's temple is just a group of people who meet to the name of the lord Jesus.

All this is indeed very mysterious but it is God Who is at work, and that is how He does things. No wonder we are told that the treasure is hidden, first in the earth, in a field and then developed slowly over years in an oyster by a process of accretion. This last is the Pearl of Great Price which is our next and last parable to be studied.

THE PEARL OF GREAT PRICE

"Again the Kingdom of the Heavens is like unto a merchant man seeking goodly pearls; who when he had found one pearl of great price went and sold all that he had, and bought it."

The word 'pearl' occurs nine times in the New Testament. Invariably it is to do with great wealth and vast riches. The pearl is different from other precious stones in that though it is made from a mineral substance it is laid down in layers organically. There is something mysterious and exotic about the pearl for it is formed in secret in the inside of the shell of a sea creature or a freshwater mussel. It has a rare and unearthly beauty with milky, misty depths as if from another world as indeed this pearl is meant to be.

There are plenty of course and vulgar people who cannot and will not receive the things of God. We find them at all levels of society. There are, for instance, the rich and the powerful who consider themselves to be too important to lower themselves to the level of the Poor but Noble king who proclaimed His rank by entering into His city riding on a donkey.

There are the 'wise' of this world who mock at the idea of Creation and a Creator. They then loudly argue for a slow process of evolution whereby something appeared spontaneously out of nothing and then developed from single celled creatures to animals and on to humans. They strain out a gnat and swallow down a camel. Claiming to be wise and rational they believe the most fantastic fairy stories while looking down their academic noses at those who have come to know and to love the real God Who is really there.

There are also the timid who worry all the time about what other people will think about them. They do not see the truth that is under their noses. Nor do they face up to facts being afraid of those facts and so they refuse to understand that it is what God thinks which matters in the long run. But the natural man receives not the things of the Spirit of God for they are foolishness unto him, neither can he know them because they are spiritually discerned. (1Cor.2:14)

Both the merchant seeking pearls and the man who finds the treasure hid in a field are pictures of the Lord Jesus who laid aside His glory and His riches and laid down His life that He might acquire something special and of very great value. Both the Treasure and the Pearl are pictures of the thing which is so valuable that the Lord Jesus paid for it so vast a price. "Forasmuch as you know that you were not redeemed with corruptible things as silver and gold, from your vain behavior received by tradition from your fathers. But with the precious blood of Christ as of a lamb without blemish and without spot." (1Pe.1: 18,19. Heb.9:14)

Pearls, being produced by an irritation within the shells of bivalve mollusks as oysters or freshwater mussels, over a period of time, show us something of the change and development of Christians and indeed of all who come to God by the Lord Jesus, over their lives by the work of the Spirit of God.

We are, for instance, to grow, both corporately and individually, we ought not to stand still in our Christian lives. Here is what Peter tells us. "But you beloved, seeing you know these things….grow in grace and in the knowledge of our Lord and Saviour Jesus Christ. To him be glory both now and for ever." (2Pe.3: 18) Paul also tells us as follows. "Be not conformed to this world, but be transformed by the renewing of your mind, that you may prove what is that good and acceptable and perfect will of God." (Rom 12: 2)

These changes happen by our cooperation with the Spirit of God. God also disciplines us as children for we have a lot to learn and sometimes we are foolish and often disobedient. Again it is God's grace that He deals with us in these ways. And always for our good. (See Heb.12:4-11)

There are also two wider senses in which these principles may be applied. We ourselves receive God's discipline and he urges us to grow. However it is also clear that This also applies to the nation of Israel.(See chapters 10 and 11 of Romans) There is also a further application in that God is also dealing with the nations as a whole and one day they also will be saved and at peace, having peace with God through our Lord Jesus Christ.

Israel is also 'a pearl of great price'. Moses recounted their past history and challenged them to learn from it. First he wrote. "Did ever people hear the voice of God speaking out of the midst of the fire as thou hast heard and live? Or has God assayed to go and take Him a nation from the midst of a nation, by testings, by signs, and by wonders, and by war and by a mighty hand and a stretched out arm, and by great terrors according to all that the Lord your God did for you in Egypt before your eyes." (Deut.4: 33-35) He then wrote showing the reason for all this and a general principle regarding His dealings with all nations and with the Body of Christ, the Church. "That you might know that the Lord, He is God, there is none else beside Him." (Loc.cit.v36)

Even after this they lapsed into Idolatry though the books of Judges and of Ruth show us that there were those who faithfully turned to God and followed His ways. Finally, after they returned from the Babylonian captivity they had learned to deplore the worship of idols, but only lapsed into the sins of Phariseeism and Sadduceeism. Eventually after great trials they will finally mourn for Him whom they pierced. Then peace will indeed come to the earth and the whole universe will be blest.

They will finally be able to take the place God originally intended for them as the head and not the tail of the nations. "And it shall come to pass, if thou shalt hearken diligently unto the voice of the Lord thy God to observe and do all His commandments, which I command thee this day, that the Lord thy God shall set thee on high above all nations of the earth." (Deut.28:1)

Pearls develop gradually, the longer they stay in the fleshy mantle of the oyster the larger and, hopefully, the more beautiful they grow. The treasure that was hidden was just that. The discoverer simply hid it again then bought the field. Here the pearl is one of exceptional value and is growing and goes on growing in the depths, hidden from the eyes of the world, the ignorant and the uncaring. One day that pearl will be complete. It will have reached the finality of its growth and of its lustrous loveliness. That is when the merchantman finds it and, having sold all his stock of precious things, buys this one whose value is above that of all the others. One day soon the church which is the body of Christ will be complete, that is when the rich merchant who has sacrificed his all to gain the priceless one will take it home with him. Still as yet the pearl still grows. It will go on growing until it is ready. There may not be much time left.

As with the church, so it is with Israel. They will go through the terrible storms of the tribulation. Just as the sea which surrounds the pearl is never at rest so the gales of anti-Israel hatred are blowing and getting stronger every day, day by day, week by week, month by month and year by year. "The wicked are like the trouble sea when it cannot rest, whose waters cast up mire and dirt. There is no peace says my God to the wicked." (Is.57: 20,21) In particular Daniel and Zechariah see the nations as striving with God and with His people and so becoming instruments of His purposes to discipline and to shape both the Christians in this age and Israel through the ages. "I saw in my vision by night and behold, the four winds of the heaven strove upon the great sea. And four great beasts came up from the sea diverse one from

100

another."(Dan.7: 2,3) Zechariah also sees these beasts, the four great world empires as four horns which are, "the horns which have scattered Judah, Israel and Jerusalem." (Zech.1: 18,19)

So through the long and bloodstained pages of world history God has been preparing His people, who are His temple, for Himself and to be with Him for ever. He allows the fury of the nations to be vented on them but this only serves to strengthen them and to make them better and wiser. The two parables give us two similar aspects of this preparation process and we see God at work and one day we shall share the honour and the glory, the joy and the bliss of the presence and the love of God in ways we only but dimly imagine and understand.

THE NET

"Again the Kingdom of the Heavens is like unto a net that was cast into the sea and gathered of every kind which, when it was full they drew to shore and sat down and gathered the good into vessels but cast the bad away." (v. 47)

There is a similarity here with the parable of the tares. There is good and bad growing together, wheat with tares and there are good fish and bad fish in the sea. As the net is hauled in then the good and the bad are caught together. It can be argued that the whole of these parables forms a unity each one contributing a different view of the whole or parts of the whole. The whole, as we are often told is 'more than the sum of its parts'.

However this, being God's Word, it does have a perfection to it and the different pictures we get do make a coherent whole. We also see a development in that the first parable, that of the Sower gives us a general picture of what is going on all the time but then leads us to see how the good seed grows and is eventually reaped. We are also shown the dangers which Satan sows among the good and how all is dealt with at the very end, at the reaping at harvest time. This is when, finally the children of God and the children of the Devil are finally separated.

The parables of the treasure and of the pearl tell us about the growth of the good seed and emphasise the work of the Lord Jesus in giving all He had. They show us that those who love Him are destined to eternal glory and bliss. It may be that the questions of predestination and of election come up when considering this subject. All this depends on God's foreknowledge shown us in the parables of the man finding the treasure in the field or among the pearls. We can then apply Romans chapter eight which says. "For whom He did foreknow, He also did predestinate to be conformed to the image of His Son." (Rom.8: 28-30 cf. Eph.1:5, 11, 12)

We are not predestined to be saved but to glory because we are already saved. God knows the future; He knows the end from the beginning. Peter confirms this saying. "Elect, according to the foreknowledge of God the Father, through sanctification of the Spirit unto obedience and sprinkling of the blood of Jesus Christ." (1Pe.1:2)

It has already been pointed out that the first four form a coherent whole as do the last three and this is the way the number seven is make up with a four and a three. The four is the universal number and three as the number of revelation of God and of the Resurrection. That last, of course being the full revelation of the Deity of the Lord Jesus.

Commentators may refer to the net as, 'the Gospel net' which in a way it is. However this tends to restrict the scope of the parable in the minds of hearers or readers. None of the parables in this section of Matthew have only this Age of Grace in view. Their scope is much wider and they contain general principles concerning the dealings of God with this world and the peoples of this world. The parables show us many facets of the Kingdom of the Heavens, how it was, how it is now and how it will be.

The book of Daniel shows us something of the angelic administration. The Watchers bring down the pride of Nebuchadnezzar but preserve his kingdom and he is allowed to be restored after seven years of humiliation. He is forced to admit that. "The Most High rules in the kingdom of men and gives and gives it to whomsoever He will and sets up over it the basest of men." (Dan.4:17)The dream which warned the King of this punishment was interpreted by Daniel. It was of a 'great tree' a prophetic picture of the King Himself. It is of course well worth comparing this to the parable of the mustard seed, there are close parallels.

There are predatory birds sheltering in its branches as there are predatory and domestic animals underneath sheltering in the shade of the tree. Here again we learn much about the administration of God in the Heavenlies. It is also a battle ground of opposing forces. The net is similar. We see how the Devil sows darnel (tares or false wheat) among the wheat seeds in order to undermine the teaching and devotion of the saints. The churches are the same. False teachers and false prophets are attracted to them. The net is dragged to the shore with all these in it. It has good and it has bad.

It is the purpose of Satan to infiltrate his own agents into the churches so they can undermine them. There are lots of religious people but only a few Christians. "Beware of false prophets," wrote Matthew, quoting the Lord Jesus. "Which come to you in sheep's clothing, but inwardly they are ravening wolves." (Mt.7:15) Paul in the same way warned the elders of the church at Ephesus. "For I know this that after my departing shall grievous wolves enter in among you not sparing the flock. Also, of your own selves shall men arise speaking perverse things to draw away disciples after them." (Acts 20:28-31)

Any serious reader of the Bible will know that this is always the case. Time and time again men and women too arise among the people of God who have their own selfish agendas. Zephaniah, for instance, wrote of the "oppressing city". This was not Nineveh nor was it Babylon as one might have expected. No! It was Jerusalem and the prophet went on to detail who these bad men were and what they were guilty of. "Her princes within her are roaring lions. Her judges," he wrote, "are evening wolves." Then of the prophets he said, they "are light and treacherous persons," and then went on to condemn the priests, saying. "Her priests have polluted the sanctuary. They have done violence to the law." (Zeph. 3:3) To this agrees Jeremiah who observed. "The prophets prophecy falsely, and the priests bear rule by their means. And My people love to have it so." (Jer.5: 30,31)

This was true in the days of these prophets, Jeremiah and Zephaniah. It was also true when John the Baptist, then the Lord Jesus, called the Pharisees, "a generation of vipers". (Mt.3:7. 12:34) So what reason might we have for suggesting it is not true today? There is no reason at all. We have men dressed up in garish pagan robes professing themselves to be priests of the Lord when only true born again humble Christians can be priests.

We have people loving the limelight pushing themselves into the public eye as 'leaders' when they do not even know God. We have theologians who do not understand a word of the Bible and as blind leaders of the blind drag others down into the mire with themselves. And we have evangelists whose purpose is self–advertising, and whose skill is in making money by appeals for gifts to which the gullible respond. All the while the Bible is reminding us that, "But my God shall supply all your needs according to His riches in glory by Christ Jesus." (Philip.4:19) In a previous verse in the same chapter of this letter, Paul councils: "Be careful for nothing, but in everything, by prayer and supplication with thanksgiving, let your requests be known unto God." (v6) The principle of not sending out begging letters could not be clearer.

Here are the tares! Here are the bad fish! Here are all the false teacher and false prophets which are to be cast away and burned. We see how deeply they have insinuated themselves into the sects and systems of Christendom and how the people think they are the reality of godliness when in actual fact they are ravening wolves. Truly the parables also have their application today but men do not

105

understand that and interpret them according to their own misplaced and misunderstood ideas.

As the harvest of the land so the harvest of the sea. "The bad are cast away." (Mt.13:48) Just so the tares are burned. This is in the end of the age. "As therefore the tares are gathered and burned in the fire, so shall it be in the end of this age. The Son of |Man shall send forth His angels and they shall gather out of His Kingdom all things that (cause to) stumble and them which do iniquity and shall cast them into the furnace of fire, there shall be wailing and gnashing of teeth." (Mt.13:40-42)

The symbolism of the sea is important. First it stresses that the Lord Jesus saves wicked men and not the self-righteous. Isaiah tells us that: "The wicked are like the troubled sea, when it cannot rest. Whose waters cast up mire and dirt." (57:20,21) and the Lord Jesus stated: "I am not come to call the righteous but sinners to repentance." (Matthew 9:13) However the message goes out to everyone. Ezekiel pits it another way when he warns the watchman to sound the warning anyway, "whether they hear or whether they forbear." (Ch.33) So the net catches may for, "many are called but few chosen" (Mt.20:16. 22:14)

For the glorious ending we may go back to the earlier part of the chapter. "Then shall the righteous shine forth as the sun in the Kingdom of their father. Who has ears to hear let him hear. (Mt. 13:13)

Thus it is that at last the treasure and the Pearl shall be revealed in all their acquired glory and beauty. Then at last shall the whole creation rejoice, shine, shout and sing. "For the earnest expectation of the creation waits for the manifestation of the Sons of God....Because the creation itself also shall be delivered from the bondage of corruption into the glorious liberty of the children of God" (Rom.8:19,21)

Not only will the Lord Jesus be revealed in all the fullness of His Might and His Glory, but Israel too shall be what it was always intended to be. We also shall, "shine forth as the sun". Everything in the whole creation shall rejoice and be what God had intended all along. Satan will be bound then cast into the lake of fire. At the very end of this creation God will put all things right; He will make all things new. "And God Himself shall be with them and be their God. And God shall wipe away all tears from their eyes and there shall be no more death, neither sorrow, nor crying, neither shall there be any more pain for the former things are passed away."

But the good, the righteous, those who are saved by Precious Blood, shall shine all the more brightly because of the evil. This is so partly because they have come through the world of evil and have triumphed. It is also because we see some who hear the welcoming words of the Lord Jesus. "Come you blessed of My Father, inherit the kingdom prepared for you from the foundation of the world." (Mt.18: 34) And the terrible contrast will be with His words to the lawless and wicked. "Depart from Me, you cursed, into everlasting fire, prepared for the Devil and his angels." (Mt.25: 41) This is the judgment of the nations whose fate will be determined by their attitudes and actions regarding God's people, that is first Israel and then all who reject the mark of the beast. "He will separate one from another." (25:31ff) While there is in this world a separation between the righteous and the lawless, in the age to come the contrasting fates will be that much more marked.

"And He that sat upon the throne said. 'Behold I make all things new'" (Rev 21:3-5) So it is with the net Everything is brought in together. This is the judgment. Then everything is separated. It is God's work at the end of the age. Everything and everyone is brought face to face with God in the person of the Lord Jesus Christ and then comes the terrible separation. Here is how John in his vision saw it all. "And I saw a Great White Throne, and Him that sat on it from Whose Face the earth and the heaven fled away and there was found no place for them. And I saw the dead, small and great stand before God. And the books were opened and another book was opened which is the Book of Life and the dead were judged out of those things which were written in the books according to their works. And the sea gave up the dead which were in it and death and Hades delivered up the dead which were in them and they were judged every man according to their works. And death and Hades were cast into the Lake of Fire. This is the second death. And whoever was not found written in the Book of Life was cast into the Lake of Fire."

END NOTE

If you have found this book interesting, or even if you have not CRF Publishers request that you·go to Amazon and rate and review it. Please be honest and tell us your thoughts.

Again we would like to keep in touch ad to send you a monthly news letter. Please go to our website, www.crfpublishers.co.uk and click on the invitation to sign up to our Newsletter. There is also more news about CRF on our Face Book page. These tell you about our books and any editing or renewing we may be doing as well as news about new publications. We publish expository books such as this one, then works on biography, philosophy, poetry and short stories.

If you are an aspiring writer or publisher we may be able to help you about getting you books published. We do not at present offer a proof reading service but we may be able to find someone to undertake that particularly challenging task. We may also be able to put you in touch with book illustrators and artists.

We look forward to hearing from you.

God bless

CRF Publishers

Books by Roger Penney

The Afterlife and the Otherworld

Another Counsellor

Dry Bones

First Century Close-Ups

The Girl on the Bus and Other stories

Herod: Commander, Builder and Statesman

Jesus in Islam

The Minor Prophets: Volume One

The Minor Prophets: Volume Two

More First Century Close –Ups

Mow: The Story of a Piratical Tom Cat

Poems of Earth Sky and Beyond

The Seven Parables of the Kingdom

A Simple Man's Guide to the Republic of Plato

A Simple Man's Guide to the Last days of Socrates

A Simple Man's Guide to Nietzsche

A Smack in the Mouth (Poems)

16288703R00062

Printed in Great Britain
by Amazon